Inclusive Practice
in the Lifelong Learning Sector

Achieving **QTLS**

Inclusive Practice
in the Lifelong Learning Sector

Sharon Powell and Jonathan Tummons

LearningMatters

First published in 2011 by Learning Matters Ltd

British Library Cataloguing in Publication Data
A CIP record for this book is available from the British Library.

ISBN: 978 0 85725 102 2

This book is also available in the following ebook formats:
Adobe ebook ISBN: 978 0 85725 104 6
EPUB ebook ISBN: 978 0 85725 103 9
Kindle ISBN: 978 0 85725 105 3

Cover design by Topics
Text design by Code 5
Project management by Deer Park Productions, Tavistock
Typeset by PDQ Typesetting Ltd, Newcastle under Lyme
Printed and bound in Great Britain by Bell & Bain Ltd, Glasgow

Learning Matters Ltd
20 Cathedral Yard
Exeter EX1 1HB
Tel: 01392 215560
info@learningmatters.co.uk
www.learningmatters.co.uk

Mixed Sources
Product group from well-managed forests and other controlled sources
www.fsc.org Cert no. TT-COC-002769
© 1996 Forest Stewardship Council
FSC

Contents

The authors

Sharon Powell has worked at Teesside University since 2004, after working as a lecturer in teacher education in the FE sector. She is an adult literacy subject specialist teacher with specific expertise in this area and in training teachers to work with students with learning difficulties and/or disabilities. In addition, she has further expertise in the assessment of dyslexia and the delivery of teacher training/education programmes specific to working with dyslexic adults.

Jonathan Tummons has worked in higher education since 1995. He took up a post as senior lecturer in education at Teesside University in 2009 after six years as a lecturer in teacher education in the FE sector. As a consultant, he has contributed to programmes for schools broadcast by Channel 4. Jonathan is currently completing an ESRC-funded PhD at the University of Lancaster, researching the assessment of trainee teachers in the learning and skills sector.

Acknowledgements

Sharon: There are a number of people I would like to thank for helping me in all sorts of ways to complete this book. My co-author Jonathan Tummons, for helping to keep me motivated and inspiring me. My good friend Sabrina Patenaude, who is the best unpaid researcher I have ever known, and also an inspiration. My two great friends Dawn Parker and Samantha Lucke, just for being there. Eleanor Glynn, a great friend and colleague, for reading some of the text through and saying that I was talking sense. My husband Rob, for sitting and watching me write night after night without complaining, and finally my family, for understanding why I was often distracted and distant during the writing of this book.

Jonathan: Thanks as always to past students at Yorkshire Coast College, York College and especially Leeds Thomas Danby. Thanks also to colleagues and friends past and present: John Aston, Liz Atkins, Suzanne Blake, Jane Brooke, Vicky Duckworth, Roy Fisher, Eleanor Glynn, Clive Hedges, Ewan Ingleby, Dawn Joyce, Gaynor Mount, Nena Skrbic, Dean Starkey. It has been a privilege to write this book with Sharon. And especially, as always, thank you to Jo, Alex and Ellie. Finally, I would like to dedicate this book to my aunt, Judy Hulse, who during her career has helped many learners with dyslexia, of all ages, to achieve both personally and academically.

Introduction

This book is intended to help all those who are currently working towards a teaching qualification that is accredited by Lifelong Learning UK (LLUK). You may already be working as a teacher or trainer in a further education college, and studying for your professional qualifications on a part-time, in-service basis. Alternatively, you may be studying for your qualification on a full-time basis, and may be about to embark on, or are already engaged on, a teaching placement. You may be employed, or seeking employment, as a tutor in adult or community education, provided by a local education authority or by organisations such as the Workers' Educational Association (WEA). You may be working as a trainer or instructor in the health sector, or in the police or fire services. These varied contexts are all covered by the LLUK standards, and practitioners in these areas are all eligible for LLUK accreditation.

This is not primarily a theoretical work. Inclusive practice is an area of significant theoretical and philosophical study: this book is not intended to be part of that particular body of literature. However, there are a few occasions when a focus on current research is desirable, and the references provided will allow those with a taste for theory to explore further. Essentially, this book is intended to provoke action as well as thought: the activities within this book, often underpinned by case studies that are composite forms of real-life experiences that we have encountered in adult education centres, further education colleges and in community-based education and training settings, are designed to facilitate the application of the ideas and issues discussed in the real world of the teacher or trainer.

Meeting National Standards

From 1 January 2005 a new organisation, Lifelong Learning UK (LLUK), began operating as the body responsible for – among other things – the professional development of all employees in the field of lifelong learning. LLUK was responsible for the new occupational standards that appear in this book until early 2011, when responsibility for the standards, and the debates over how these might be reformed, was transferred to the Learning and Skills Improvement Service (LSIS).

How to use this book

This book may be read from cover to cover, in one sitting, or it may be read on a chapter-by-chapter basis over a longer period of time. Each chapter is designed so that it can be read in isolation, as and when needed, although references to topics covered in other chapters will be found from time to time.

Within each chapter are a number of features that are designed to engage the reader, and provoke an active response to the ideas and themes that are covered. Objectives at the start of each chapter set the scene, and then the appropriate LLUK professional standards for that chapter are listed. In some places, an activity will be found. These activities have been designed to facilitate the practical application of some of the issues covered. The case studies and real-life examples in this book are drawn from a variety of teaching and training contexts, as a reflection of the diversity of the learning and skills sector as a whole. Finally, each chapter finishes with suggestions for what to do next. A small number of sources, books, journal articles and websites are recommended at the end of each chapter. These lists are by no means exhaustive, however: the featured items have been chosen because of their suitability and value for use and study by trainee teachers in the learning and skills sector.

A definition of inclusive practice

Inclusive practice is a far-reaching, nuanced term that can mean a number of things to different people. Sometimes it is narrowly equated with disability awareness, for example, or with making adjustments for students with specific learning needs. In this book, we understand inclusive practice as being an approach to teaching and learning that endeavours to encourage the fullest participation of learners. It also implies a commitment to avoid the opposite; that is to say, it implies that tutors work within an ethical framework that recognises and respects equality and diversity, and the potential for all learners to take part. As we proceed through the book, different aspects of this definition will be explored in more depth.

And finally

We are always pleased to hear from trainee teachers about our writing or our research. If you would like to get in touch, please email Jonathan at j.tummons@tees.ac.uk, or you can look for us on facebook, (search "Sharon Powell and Jonathan Tummons").

1
Defining inclusion

By the end of this chapter you should:

- have a developing understanding of the terms, 'inclusion' and 'inclusive practice';
- begin to develop your own ideological and philosophical viewpoint about inclusion and inclusive teaching practices;
- begin to be able to evaluate the personal, political, economic and social influences that can impact upon access to further education and training;
- have a developing ability to relate your growing understanding of inclusion issues and inclusive practice to the planning of your teaching and learning activities;
- be able to evaluate the constraints and some of the issues around providing an inclusive curriculum.

Professional Standards

This chapter relates to the following Professional Standards:

Professional Values:

AS 2 Learning, its potential to benefit people emotionally, intellectually, socially and economically, and its contribution to community sustainability.

AS 3 Equality, diversity and inclusion in relation to learners, the workforce and the community.

Professional Knowledge and Understanding:

AK 3.1 Issues of equality, diversity and inclusion.

DK 1.1 How to plan appropriate, effective, coherent and inclusive learning programmes that promote equality and engage with diversity.

Professional Practice:

AP 3.1 Apply principles to evaluate and develop own practice in promoting equality and inclusive learning and engaging with diversity.

Inclusion and inclusive practice

In this chapter, the key terms 'inclusion' and 'inclusive practice' are introduced, explored and then critiqued. This chapter aims to provide readers not only with a thorough understanding of the practical meaning of 'inclusion' and 'inclusive practice', but also a critical account of how these meanings have been formed. The chapter will encourage us to critically evaluate how inclusive our teaching practices are and will help us to reflect upon when and how we might adapt our classroom practices to make learning as accessible as possible. Before we discuss inclusion and inclusive practice, it is worth taking some time to reflect upon who our students are and where they have come from.

Before progressing through this chapter, spend some time reflecting upon who your students are. Try to identify what their reasons might be for attending their particular programme of study and make a list of these. Following this, try to categorise the reasons as personal (I want to do the programme), professional (I need it for my job), social (I want to have fun and make new friends), economic (I want to improve my employment prospects and earn more money) or political (I have to attend a programme of education or my benefits will be cut).

As tutors and trainers it is important that we have an understanding of the reasons (or drivers) people have for attending programmes of education and training. The next section of this chapter spends some time exploring this.

Who are the learners and what are the drivers that lead them to attend Further Education?

The student body is continually changing; who they are, where they have come from, their reasons for being in education, what they need/want to learn and why. More often than not, the students we find sitting in front of us are just as likely to have arrived as a result of external influences, such as political, social and/or economic drivers, as for any intrinsic, internal desire to learn. The current 14–19 education and training agenda means that the majority of the students we teach may be on vocational programmes that exist to provide trained workers for industry on the completion of the course of learning, or we may be delivering training programmes to adults in work who need the qualification for their job and are there 'because they have to be'. Both of these groups of learners are different in many ways, for example, age, motivations, where they are in their careers, why they are on the programme of learning in the first place, but they have one thing in common: they are all attending education and training partly due to external influences. As tutors and trainers we cannot underestimate the influence that, for example, government policy decisions have on the demographic of the student body. Why does the student demographic change so much and why do we need to know about it? As trainee tutors and trainers it is important for us to be aware that as our careers progress the profile of the learners we teach will change, and if we are to remain inclusive in our practices our approaches to learning and teaching should change with them. Because of this it's worth spending a little time looking at some examples of how further education (FE) provision has changed over the past 18 years or so as it will help us to contextualise what is happening today and will also help to demonstrate how government policy changes education and training provision in the UK.

The 1990s

The incorporation of Colleges of Further Education

The incorporation of FE colleges in 1993 led to the removal of Local Education Authority (LEA) control over funding to colleges and the introduction of The Further Education Funding Council (FEFC), a non-departmental public body of the Department for Education and Skills (DfES). This effectively centralised control over funding to colleges. This action had significant influence on the curriculum offer colleges would make as:

- colleges no longer had to agree the programmes they would deliver with the LEA and be funded from the delivery of these. What was to be delivered locally was to be brought into a centralised funding system;
- it introduced the marketplace into FE with colleges often choosing to offer the programmes which attracted the most FEFC funding. These were often the same programmes as their rivals and therefore they were in direct competition with each other to attract the same students. Colleges had to think very carefully about competitors and how they could sell their programmes most effectively to recruit students. They also looked at niche markets which would attract FEFC funding but were specialist in some way, thus reducing the potential for competition;
- it led to a marked reduction in programmes that were considered 'recreational'. Programmes such as cake decorating and flower arranging attracted little or negligible FEFC funding, leading to colleges often removing them from their curriculum offer, or if they were offered, they had a significant fee attached. This changed the face of FE provision as colleges naturally gravitated towards programmes that would provide them with the most financial gain. As a result of this, FE became much more sharply focused on providing vocational training (where the funding was) and less focused on recreational programmes. What did still exist under this new regime was funding to provide programmes of education for learners with learning difficulties and/or disabilities. This funding was used by colleges to offer discrete programmes of learning. At this point in time the inclusion of learners with moderate to severe learning difficulties into mainstream provision in post-compulsory education was uncommon.

The Inclusive Learning agenda

The Tomlinson Report (1996), or *Inclusive Learning*, played a key role in the post-compulsory sector's widening participation agenda. The Tomlinson Report investigated widening participation specifically for learners with learning difficulties or disabilities. Tomlinson found that students with special educational needs were underachieving in the post-compulsory sector; were unable to access the wider curriculum; and were, for the most part, lacking in confidence, possibly because of their previous school experience of education and learning. The Report found that learners with learning difficulties or disabilities were historically excluded from mainstream opportunities in the post-compulsory sector. It also found that this form of exclusion affected the culture of learning providers such as FE colleges. Tomlinson recommended that the responsibility should be on the educational institution to empathise with and respond to the individual, and to address the needs of that individual learner. Among the Report's recommendations was a requirement that institutions should publish their own disability statements, with information regarding entry and openness of access, which should operate regardless of age, gender, ethnicity or disability. The Report envisaged that such a focus on inclusive learning would improve the quality of learner experience for students with difficulties or disabilities and, indeed, change the culture of educational establishments by focusing on planning with, and supporting the needs of, individuals.

The Widening Participation agenda

Widening participation first became a major focus of attention for FE colleges with the publication of *Learning Works* by Helena Kennedy QC in June 1997. This paper was developed in response to the FEFC drive to promote access to FE for people who do not participate in education and training, but who could benefit from it. This put widening participation firmly at the centre of FE training from 1997 onwards, as colleges that could demonstrate they had recruited effectively from these under-represented areas were provided with additional funding. Therefore, it was (and still is) in an FE college's best interest to be actively engaged in the widening participation agenda.

2000 onwards

The Skills for Life Strategy
In 2001 came the Skills for Life Strategy, the Labour government's drive to develop the basic communication, literacy and numeracy skills of 2.5 million adults between 2001 and 2011. This was a major government initiative which was extremely high profile. TV and radio adverts were used to promote the strategy, access to basic skills classes was free of charge, there was flexible access to the programmes and additional money for innovations in delivering basic skills provision to those potential learners who were 'hard to reach'. As with all high-priority government education initiatives, the financial incentives to institutions delivering good-quality provision in these areas were high. The strategy would build on the inclusive learning and widening participation initiatives and once again changed the balance of the student demographic. Target groups for the Skills for Life Strategy were:

- the unemployed and people on benefits, to assist them in developing skills that would help to get them back into work;
- prisoners, in order to raise their employment opportunities on leaving prison;
- criminals supervised in the community;
- public sector employees;
- people in employment but classed as having low skills;
- young adults;
- parents;
- people living in disadvantaged communities;
- other groups at risk from exclusion as a result of having poor basic skills.

The 14–19 agenda
More recently other government initiatives have influenced the student profile of those accessing FE. For example, the change in FE being focused on the 16-plus age group to encompass students from the age of 14, the advent of the vocational diploma and more recently an increasing focus on the vocational training of learners in the 16–19 age range have once again changed the profile of the FE curriculum offer.

Higher Education in FE settings
It is also worth mentioning that in the last decade FE colleges' collaboration with Higher Education Institutions (HEIs), in order to enable them to offer the higher level FEHQ awards (level 4 and 5 primarily, such as Foundation Degrees), has increased. This means that more students than ever are studying higher education qualifications in FE colleges. HEIs work within The Higher Education Funding Council for England's Strategic Plan and aspects of this plan relate to the widening participation agenda. HEIs have to demonstrate that they are providing ongoing opportunities for different social groups and under-represented groups to access higher education, specifically disabled students, mature students, women and men and all ethnic groups, whether they are attending higher education at the university or with a partner college.

The 2010 change of government
When the Conservative-led coalition government was formed following the May 2010 election, the country was warned of unprecedented cuts in public spending, and education has been hit particularly hard. The removal of the cap on higher education student tuition fees and the abolition of the Education Maintenance Allowance (EMA) designed to support learners from poor backgrounds in accessing FE are examples of these. What impact will the removal of the EMA have?

In 2010 the coalition government announced the withdrawal of the EMA commencing academic year 2011. This led to many student protests across the country in early 2011, with many students reporting that without the £30 a week allowance they could not afford to stay in FE. The government argue that only 12% of students reported that they would have to leave education as a result of the withdrawal of the EMA and that 88% of students would remain in education regardless. The government concluded that this was too high a percentage of wastage, i.e. money that did not have to be spent to keep students in FE. However, the Institute for Fiscal Studies found that the EMA significantly increased participation rates in post-16 education among young adults who were eligible to receive it. In particular, it increased the proportion of eligible 16-year-olds staying in education from 65% to 69%, and increased the proportion of eligible 17-year-olds in education from 54% to 61%. Based on these impacts, and on estimates of the financial benefits of additional education taken from elsewhere in the economics literature, their study concluded that the costs of providing EMA were likely to be exceeded in the long run by the higher wages that its recipients would go on to enjoy. If the purpose of EMA is to increase participation in education, then the higher the deadweight, the less valuable it will be. The question is: to what extent does the 'wasted' spending on those whose behaviour was unaffected offset the beneficial effect of the spending on those whose behaviour was affected? A simple cost–benefit analysis suggests that even taking into account the level of deadweight that was found, the costs of EMA are completely offset.

Do you think that the removal of the EMA will prevent students from accessing FE? Is this promoting or restricting inclusion to learning in your opinion and why?

In 2011 and onwards, different drivers are at work that will once again influence the profile of students accessing FE training, and once more teachers and trainers in the Lifelong Learning sector will have to adapt their practices to meet this new agenda.

Inclusive practices in teaching and learning defined

We have briefly looked at some of the outside influences that affect who might access, or be included in, FE but now we need to look more closely at defining inclusion and inclusive practices for those learners on programmes of learning who we are responsible for teaching. The next section of this chapter focuses on the pedagogical aspects of inclusion and inclusive practice.

REFLECTIVE TASK

What is your understanding of the terms 'inclusion' and 'inclusive practice' from a pedagogical (or teaching and learning) perspective? Spend some time thinking about your teaching practices. Write down your own definition of what inclusive practice is.

The following 'theory focus' provides a summary of definitions of inclusive practice taken over a span of 14 years. You will see that they have some similarities that you might reflect upon. Was your definition similar to any of the following definitions?

THEORY FOCUS **THEORY** FOCUS **THEORY** FOCUS **THEORY** FOCUS **THEORY** FOCUS

Tomlinson (1996) defines 'inclusive learning' as being the greatest degree of match or fit between how learners learn best, what they need and want to learn, and what is required by the sector. Tummons (2010) argues that 'inclusive practice' is thinking about delivering teaching and the curricula in a way that enables learners to access it to the best of their ability. Petty (2004) discusses differentiation (i.e. adapting your classroom practices to promote inclusion) as accommodating individual differences by adopting strategies for learning that ensure access to learning for all. Ingleby and Powell (2010) define inclusive practice as the use of a variety of differentiated approaches to teaching and learning in the classroom in order to deliver the curricula content in such a way as to promote access to learning for as many learners as possible.

Therefore, inclusive practice can be seen as adapting what we do to make learning accessible. It suggests some activity or 'action' needs to be taken to ensure that inclusion can take place; for example, inclusive actions might include:

- the removal of physical barriers that prevent access to our classroom, such as providing a ramp for wheelchair users to enable access;
- adapting some of our teaching practices and/or teaching and learning resources to enable a partially sighted learner or a learner with a specific learning difficulty to participate fully in learning activities;
- adapting our teaching and learning strategies to differentiate for the different speeds that learners in our classrooms work at;
- the realisation that some of our learners may need more support than others and putting appropriate mechanisms in place to meet this need, for example an appropriate and flexible tutorial system;
- making learning accessible from outside the classroom as well as in it. Most FE colleges have a virtual learning environment, and the innovative use of a VLE can make learning accessible to learners around the clock.

REFLECTIVE TASK

Ask yourself the following questions:

1. How often do I reflect upon my class teaching and learning strategies in relation to the progress in learning of each individual learner within that class?
2. If I feel that a learner is falling behind or failing, what reasons might there be and what can or should I do about it?
3. How do I know if a learner is achieving his/her full potential and what can I put in place to try to facilitate this?
4. What constraints do I have to work within, and how will these, if at all, affect how inclusive in my practice I can be?

Consider the following case studies: they are both about trainee teachers who have been in teaching placement for a relatively short space of time in FE colleges. In Case Study 1 Mike is delivering an HNC level 3 Sports Studies programme and in Case Study 2 Simon is delivering an NVQ level 3 Child Care programme. Both trainee teachers are in the very early stages of their professional formation and have not yet established a set ideology or philosophy of their own approaches to learning and teaching. Both of these trainee teachers are struggling in their own way, but their experiences are very different.

CASE STUDY 1

Mike is embarking upon a career change, moving from working at a local sports centre into teaching. Mike is interested in teaching sports studies and gained a place on a pre-service Professional Graduate Certificate in Education (PGCE) at the local college of FE. In his previous job at the sports centre he observed some of the training and mentoring that took place, which was very casual and unstructured. In addition to this, when Mike did his own degree ten years ago, his memory of this time was of teaching methods where the tutor delivered material in a lecture and there may have been a seminar session, but the onus was on Mike to learn the materials and pass the assessments, i.e. to learn mostly on his own. As a result of this, Mike begins his teaching practice by delivering 'chalk and talk' didactic teaching sessions, encouraging students to make notes from his teaching and then use the library to learn more about the subject in-depth. He is also very strict about when students can access tutorial sessions with him and this has reduced access to him for some learners. This doesn't concern him as he feels that as adults they should be capable of self-study and learning from each other. Mike thinks all is going well until his PGCE teaching practice assessor provides him with feedback from his first teaching practice observation which is poor; and his college mentor, that same week, also tells him that some students are very unhappy with the experience they are having in the classroom and are feeling very unsupported in their studies in general.

CASE STUDY 2

Simon has worked for some years in Early Years settings as a teaching assistant in a primary school. He spent some time informally helping to mentor Foundation Degree students on an Early Years programme and decided that he would like to change the direction of his career from working with children to working with adults. Simon decided to join a pre-service PGCE course at his local college. In doing so he was taking a gamble as he gave up his full-time job to do the programme. He was motivated and enthusiastic and was looking forward to his teaching practice. Simon is very conscientious, does his research and when it comes to planning his teaching sessions he feels he is well read and organised. On completion of his first teaching observation he gets some good feedback; he has set good aims and objectives and has prepared a range of teaching learning and assessment activities using a variety of techniques. However, he is advised that some students, the ones that are perhaps less able and slower in completing the tasks, are taking more of his attention than others and that the other students are in danger of becoming demotivated and bored as they sit for quite long spells with nothing to do. Simon is not sure how to tackle this imbalance, so continues with the same strategy. The problem he now has is that the behaviour of the more able learners has disintegrated. On completing tasks they become noisy and disruptive and this is taking his attention from the slower learners, compounding the problem. This also begins to spill over into his work outside the classroom, with the more needy students emailing him and telephoning him almost daily and demanding more of his time for tutorial support than he expects, probably because they are not getting the opportunity for support and feedback in the class. This has become such an issue that he is struggling in his 'work time' at placement to complete his other associated tasks and is having to take work home as a result. He knows the situation can't continue but is at a loss as to what to do.

Case studies discussion

Mike and Simon are attending their teacher training course at the same college and are in the same 'action learning set' or 'peer session', which is set aside for them to discuss and share their teaching successes and failures in a safe environment. They discuss their relative experiences and problems with each other as well as the other members in their group. These are the observations their peers and tutors make.

The general view is that neither Mike nor Simon are being as inclusive in their practices as they could be. The issues that have arisen can be explained to some extent by students feeling that their needs are not being met, and that they are not being as fully included in the learning process as they could be.

Mike is advised to review his teaching and learning strategies. His own experiences of learning (being autonomous, taking notes, working things out for himself and listening to the lecturer) may have suited him as a learner, but he has fallen into the trap a lot of trainee teachers fall into – teaching the way he liked to learn. This means that Mike is not being as inclusive as he might be in his teaching approaches. The peers in Mike's group advise him that although he is delivering the curriculum content, he is not doing it in a way that will make it accessible to the majority of learners in his group. His peers advise him to try different teaching and learning strategies in his lessons, to bring in discussion, group work and paired tasks, to watch DVDs, have quizzes, poster presentations, role plays and generally to make the learning opportunities for the learners as varied as possible. Although he still may not be meeting all the learning needs of every learner, or the 'best match' to the way each learner learns, at least he will be being a lot more inclusive in his practice than he has been, and by using a lot of different techniques he will be providing much better opportunities for the learners to access the lesson content and the learning materials in a way that is meaningful for them. By doing this he is also more likely to avoid student complaints.

Simon has a different problem. Although the strategies he is using in his sessions are varied, and he is trying to be inclusive in his approaches, he is still not meeting the needs of his learners effectively in the classroom and this has led to other issues. Simon is advised that perhaps the best way to tackle the problems in the teaching session is to consider differentiated approaches to his teaching and learning activities. Using differentiated approaches will best enable him to meet the needs of his learners. Simon's peers remind him of what a differentiated classroom is and refer back to some reading they completed as part of the programme in which they discussed Tomlinson's notion of a differentiated classroom. This emphasises that learning experiences need to be based on readiness to learn, learning interests and learning profiles. This means that the content and activities in the session and the expected learning outcomes are developed according to the varied needs of the group and the individual learners. This helps to ensure that learners are challenged and continually engaged in learning. Tomlinson goes on to discuss the advantages of a differentiated classroom, as it provides the best access to learning, promotes effectiveness of learning and encourages motivation in learning. Simon knows the learners in the group well. He knows the ones who complete work more quickly and are more able. He reflects upon what he knows about differentiated approaches and remembers that there are five main ways in which you can differentiate your teaching practice. They are: by learning outcome, by speed, by extension, by resource and by task type (Paton and Wilkins, 2009). If he tries this approach he should find himself able to spend more time with the more demanding learners in the group, as the more able learners should be engaged in learning as a result of the differentiated learning activities he plans to use each week. Simon's other problem (students demanding time outside of the classroom) should hopefully become more manageable as a result of this strategy.

Both Mike and Simon agree to report back to the group in a few weeks.

We have spent some time looking at examples and case studies. Now it is time for you to complete a practical task which will help to demonstrate how inclusive your planned approaches to teaching and learning are.

PRACTICAL TASK PRACTICAL TASK PRACTICAL TASK PRACTICAL TASK PRACTICAL TASK

Select two groups that you are currently working with that have differing profiles. Select a session plan you have devised for each group and answer the following questions about them:

1. What are the main differences in the way you have planned the sessions and why?
2. Do you think you have built in differentiated approaches to learning and teaching as well as you might, e.g. learning outcome, speed, extension, resource and task type?
3. Do you have a range of teaching and learning activities planned that will provide a variety of learning opportunities?
4. Have you planned to provide a range of assessment strategies, formative and summative as appropriate?
5. What constraints did you have to work within when planning the sessions? These might be time constraints (you might have limited time to plan and prepare for your teaching), resource constraints (the classroom you are timetabled in might not be the most ideal for what you are delivering, or the amount of money you can spend on photocopying, models or demonstration materials may be limited), organisational constraints (a standard lesson plan format that you have to use for all sessions), the requirements of any external awarding bodies (for example, some awarding bodies may only accept assessed work in a particular format for certain awards and this may constrain the strategies for assessment you can select for use)...to name a few.

Can we truly be fully inclusive in our teaching and learning practices?

As we have discussed earlier in the chapter, a truly inclusive curriculum takes account of the needs of the learners in order for them to be provided with the best opportunities to learn. Student tutors or trainers should be proactive at the planning stage in thinking about the wider implications for meeting the individual needs of the learners. However, in reality teaching practice is never as straightforward as this. A number of constraints, as indicated previously, may make it difficult for us as tutors or trainers always to do exactly what we want to do, and more often than not, when faced with the reality of such things as limited resources and little time, a compromise is reached, a trade-off between being as inclusive in our approaches as possible and what is actually achievable. However, as professional tutors or trainers we should still always strive to be as inclusive in our approaches to teaching and learning as we possibly can.

A SUMMARY OF **KEY POINTS**

In this chapter we have:

> discussed the terms 'inclusion' and 'inclusive practice' from a range of perspectives and have looked at some of the influences of FE and training provision from personal, political, social and economic viewpoints;

> evaluated issues of inclusion and inclusive practice in terms of curriculum delivery and the potential impact this might have on teaching and learning practices;

> examined some of the constraints and some of the issues around providing an inclusive curriculum for all of our learners all of the time.

We hope that this chapter has helped you to begin to develop your own ideological and philosophical viewpoint about what inclusive practice is and that it has helped to raise your awareness of the issues surrounding inclusion and inclusive practice in general.

REFERENCES AND FURTHER READING REFERENCES AND FURTHER READING

Books

Ingleby, J and Powell, S (2010) *Learning to Teach in the Lifelong Learning Sector*. London: Continuum.

Paton, A and Wilkins, M (eds) (2009) *Teaching Adult ESOL: Principles and Practice*. London: Open University Press.

Petty, G (2004) *Teaching Today – A Practical Guide*. Third edition. Cheltenham: Nelson Thornes.

Tummons, J (2010) *Becoming a Professional Tutor in the Lifelong Learning Sector*. Second edition. Exeter: Learning Matters.

Government publications

Kennedy, H (1997) *Learning Works.* London: DfEE.

The Tomlinson Report (1996) *Inclusive Learning*. London: HMSO.

The Skills for Life Strategy (2001).

Websites

The Institute of Fiscal Studies www.ifs.org.uk/

HEFCE Strategic Plan www.hefce.ac.uk/aboutus/stratplan

2
Models of disability

By the end of this chapter you should:

- have a developing understanding of medical and social models of disability;
- have a growing understanding of the implications for the two models of disability on education and training practices;
- be aware of some of the key pieces of governmental legislation that have informed the responses of educational institutions towards students with disabilities or learning difficulties.

Professional Standards

This chapter relates to the following professional standards:

Professional Values:

AS 3 Equality, diversity and inclusion in relation to learners, the workforce and the community.

FS 2 Providing support for learners within the boundaries of the teacher role.

Professional Knowledge and Understanding;

FK 1.1 Sources of information, advice, guidance and support to which learners might be referred.

FK 1.2 Internal services which learners might access.

Professional Practice:

FP 1.1 Refer learners to information on potential current and future learning opportunities and appropriate specialist support services.

Introduction

In the light of what we have discussed in the preceding chapter, it might feel somewhat artificial to be focusing, in this chapter, specifically on disability. After all, if inclusion and inclusive practice are indeed about 'more' than 'just' students with disabilities, why should issues surrounding disability be foregrounded at the expense of, for example, specific learning difficulties, or even those other dimensions of difference (such as race, gender, sexuality or social class) that also need to be part of our wider conversation about inclusive practice? Our response to this question is twofold. Firstly, as teachers and writers, we do not hold that any one of these factors is any more important than another, and all of these factors will receive coverage within this book. Secondly, however, we feel that it is not so much the issue of practical responses to working with students with seen, or unseen, disabilities that we wish to foreground in this chapter, but rather it is individual and social attitudes towards, and understandings of, disability itself that we wish to unpack. Hints and tips about how best to adjust your classroom so that a student with impaired mobility or who needs to use assistive technology are, generally speaking, straightforward to obtain. But a considered and critical discussion about how we, as teachers, understand, talk about or respond to disability – or, to put it another way, how we *construct* disability – is far less prevalent within teacher education literature for the Lifelong Learning sector.

To describe such a discussion as 'absent' might seem surprising: at first glance, many mainstream FE colleges in particular appear to be adept at accommodating students with disabilities. The inclusion within a classroom of a student who uses a wheelchair or who is supported by a British Sign Language (BSL) interpreter and a note-taker is not uncommon. Colleges, adult education providers and private training centres invariably have either a mission statement that makes reference to students with disabilities and learning difficulties, or a specific policy relating to such students, or both. Together with the demands of Ofsted inspections and legislation (such as SENDA and DDA, which will be explored more fully in Chapter 8), it might appear that a more detailed exploration of how disability is perceived, discussed and reacted to might seem superfluous. In fact, the reverse is true, and although there are many more opportunities for students with disabilities within the Lifelong Learning sector, attitudes towards such students have not changed as coherently or as profoundly as campaigning or advocacy groups might hope for.

REFLECTIVE TASK

In the following passage from his learning journal, David, a full-time teacher-training student, reflects on his experiences of working with a profoundly deaf student during his first teaching placement at a large mixed FE college. As you read, think about the ways in which David reports the experiences of the student, and think about how you might be able to inform your own behaviours or responses to a student with a disability when you meet such a student in one of your classes.

My level 3 class was pretty straightforward, but the level 2 class was very surprising. I have never seen a deaf student in a training kitchen before – I didn't think that if you were deaf you'd want to train to work in a kitchen, to be honest. But the student had a sign language interpreter and she followed him around pretty much all of the time, so that seemed to work. The tutor was good, and spent a lot of time talking to the interpreter as well, so I assumed that she managed to keep the deaf student up to date with everything that needed to be done during the practical. We were in the kitchens for two hours before the break, and then for the last hour we were in the classroom for the underpinning theory. There wasn't much to this to be honest, as it was only a level 2 course. The students spent most of their time copying some notes from the board and then putting together some supporting evidence for their portfolios. The deaf student had a note-taker for this so he just wrote the stuff down from the board and then put it in the student's file.

So what is happening here? A cursory reading of this journal entry might lead the reader to assume that 'good practice' has been established relating to the inclusion of the deaf student. A BSL interpreter was present throughout, the teacher spent a lot of time talking to the interpreter, and a note-taker was present for the theory-based part of the session. A more critical reading of the session, by contrast, raises a number of issues that can help lead our discussion towards how disability is understood, responded to and defined.

Being surprised to see a deaf student

Images of people with disabilities are relatively uncommon within the mainstream media. It may well be the case that, for example, there are no profoundly deaf chefs hosting their own television cookery programmes. But the catering and hospitality sector, in common with many other employers, counts people with disabilities among its workforce (we will return later to the catering and hospitality sector, and to a case study report of how adjustments have been made for staff with disabilities working in hotels). Just as not every student who achieves a level 2 NVQ in Beauty Therapy goes on to work in a beauty salon, so it is the case that not every student who studies for a level 2 NVQ in Catering goes on to work in a professional kitchen. But if we view such an award as a transferable qualification that serves to facilitate entry to employment, then why should the presence of a deaf student be in any way remarkable?

Talking to the BSL interpreter

Undoubtedly, it is to the tutor's credit that he spends time talking with the BSL interpreter during the session. But what would be more useful to know would be the amount of time that he spent talking to the student *through* the interpreter. It is likely that the BSL interpreter knows more about the needs of deaf students, in general, than the tutor does. Consequently, any time that the tutor can spend talking with her in order to get advice or help can only be time well spent. But the tutor also needs to be sure that he establishes and sustains a direct working relationship with the student as well, taking care to address him directly, using eye contact and gesture where appropriate, and all the while taking time to allow the interpreter to do her work as well.

Note-taking and portfolio building

If we are to assume that the assessment for this NVQ is both reliable and valid, then any students with disabilities should, as long as appropriate additional support or resources have been put in place, work towards the same assessment criteria and outcomes as all of the other students within their peer group (and examples of the different kinds of adjustments that might be made in such circumstances can be found in the following two chapters). But how appropriate, for a deaf student, are the assessment activities that are being described here? Certainly, a note-taker will help a great deal because their presence frees up the student to work with his BSL interpreter. But this support needs to be understood in the light of the fact that for the student, English is a second language: his first language is BSL, and the grammar, vocabulary and syntax of BSL are quite different from English. As such, the tutor cannot assume that any notes that he puts up on the board can be straightforwardly 'translated' into BSL by the interpreter – additional explanation may be required. The same goes for the candidate handbook that the students will all be working towards. Making sense of some of the NVQ handbooks that awarding bodies produce can be a difficult task at the best of times, let alone for students for whom English is not a first language. This is not to say that the student will not be able to work with the notes or the handbook: but this work will take more time, and this time needs to be planned for so that the student is not disadvantaged.

When writing this reflection, David has in fact recorded much that is to be commended. Many students find themselves without appropriate additional support at different stages in their learning journey. The FE college where David is on placement has done well to arrange both BSL and note-taking support. And yet there is still more to do. This is not because either the tutor or the college are doing anything 'wrong', as such. Rather, this is because of a lack of critical, reflective awareness as to the needs of the student. We have a note-taker, and this is a good thing: but these notes are being taken in a second language. We have a BSL interpreter to help the student make sense of their candidate handbook, but the same language issues apply. We have a deaf student working towards a hospitality award, and yet this still causes surprise on David's part. It seems right to locate these problematic responses somewhere in how we – as tutors and as teacher-training students – understand or *construct* notions of disability, and so it is to this that we shall now turn.

Constructing disability

How is the word 'disability' used, and what kinds of meanings are attached to it? How might teachers respond if they are told that a student with 'a disability' will be attending one of their classes? How do teachers treat disabled students, or even talk to them? Answers to questions such as these rest in part on how 'disability' is defined, how it is talked about, and even how it is explained. Or, to put it another way, it is in how ideas about disability are *constructed* that we can answer questions such as these. Constructions of disability, which as we shall see have changed dramatically over recent decades, can be thought about in a number of ways:

- in terms of how it is defined;
- in terms of the discourses that surround it (that is to say, the way that people talk about it);
- and in terms of how disability is responded to.

We shall discuss each of these in turn.

Constructing definitions of disability

One hundred years ago, the ways in which disability was defined were based on what is now termed a *medical model of disability*. That is to say, it was the medical profession (as distinct from, for the purposes of this discussion, the teaching profession) that defined both the physical and mental conditions that people who were called 'disabled' possessed. This model of disability has also been referred to as an *individual model*, as a way of stressing the fact that it was as a consequence of the individual person's possession of particular mental or physical attributes that they were defined as disabled. The disability, as a medical condition, rested solely within them. The medical model of disability has also been referred to as a *deficit model*, as a way of stressing the fact that people with disabilities were viewed as being 'less than' a 'whole person', as lacking particular physical or mental capabilities or capacities that therefore prevented them from, for example, accessing mainstream education. And it was members of the medical profession, not the education profession, who 'diagnosed' whether or not a student would benefit from attending a special school. Indeed, even the title of the relevant government legislation from 1914 that established the role of LEAs in providing for children with disabilities illustrates the attitudes prevalent at the time: the Elementary Education (*Defective* and Epileptic) Act (emphasis added).

Notwithstanding more recent criticism, the publication in 1978 of the Warnock Report signalled a significant shift in attitudes towards the education of people with physical or mental disabilities. It established criteria for assessing the needs of children based on their educational needs, rather than medical criteria. The Warnock Report also called for greater parental involvement in planning for the education of children with special educational needs (SEN) and, most importantly for the purposes of this book, for SEN provision to be extended to the FE sector as well. Thus, rather than continuing to segregate learners with disabilities in special schools, they were, wherever possible and practicable, to be *integrated* into mainstream education. However, there was no acknowledgement of any differential curricular needs on the part of such learners, and once integrated into mainstream schools (although the extent of such integration was questionable – many found themselves segregated in separate classrooms, with shared activities restricted to social settings such as school lunchtimes), they still needed to follow the mainstream curriculum.

It was not until almost 20 years later that changing definitions of disability could be found embodied within government legislation. The publication of the *Special Needs Code of Practice* by the then Department for Education and Employment in 1994, followed by the Special Educational Needs and Disability Act (2001), and the extension four years later of the Disability Discrimination Act (which was originally passed by parliament in 1995) to include coverage of educational institutions, can all be seen as resting on a quite different definition of disability, which is known as a *social model*.

CASE STUDY 1
Accessing an in-service CertEd/PGCE (PCET)

Several years ago, when we were both still working in FE colleges, one of us was teaching a CertEd/PGCE group that included a student, Linda, who had mobility problems and therefore had to use a wheelchair for much of the day. But physical access to the building where the teacher-training classes were held was only one of the several problems that she had to navigate, and it was through this process of navigation that the social model of disability could be observed. The other adjustments that we eventually made included:

- Ensuring that the tables and chairs in the classroom were arranged in such a way that, should she choose or need to do so, Linda would be able to move around the whole classroom with minimal fuss, rather than being stuck in one place. In fact, Linda, like most students, tended to sit in the same place each week as different peer groups formed within the class, but having the furniture moved did mean that she could take part fully in different small-group or buzz-group activities.
- Extending the time allowed for a break in the middle of the session, so that Linda would have time to go to the cafeteria with the other students. In the end, only an extra few minutes were required, but this did mean that she was not excluded from the more informal social activities of the group.
- Having the teacher-training books in the library re-shelved so that they were lower down: originally, some of the books were simply too high for Linda to reach. Yes, she could ask one of the staff in the library for help, but that was not the point: it took only a minor adjustment for Linda to be able to work through the books for herself.

A social model of disability works very differently to a medical model. A medical model assumes that people with disabilities cannot do particular things (such as, but not restricted to, accessing certain kinds of educational facilities) because of their disability. In this sense, their disability is the problem or the barrier that prevents them from taking part. A social model of disability turns all of this around, and instead places the barriers not within the individual person with a disability, but within the society or social world in which that person lives. Disabilities in themselves need not be barriers (although clearly not everyone gets to do everything, a debate we shall return to). The barriers are put up, more or less knowingly, by institutions – by shops, offices, employers – and by education providers as well. By being sensitive to how such barriers become established, colleges or adult education providers can improve access to both the physical spaces where courses are delivered, and to the curricula that are delivered there.

RESEARCH FOCUS RESEARCH FOCUS RESEARCH FOCUS RESEARCH FOCUS RESEARCH FOCUS

How universally applicable is the social model of disability?

In a research paper published in 2001, Anne Louise Chappell, Dan Goodley and Rebecca Lawthom drew on research that had been conducted among self-advocacy groups that represented people with learning difficulties in order to explore the ways in which such groups employed a social model of disability. They found that although disabled activist groups made significant use of a social model in articulating the perspectives of their members and campaigning over a number of different rights and access issues, people with learning difficulties had been, in essence, 'left behind' by the social model. The authors stated their case quite baldly:

> Writers committed to the social model have applied it with great enthusiasm to physical and sensory impairment, but they have neglected people with learning difficulties. [...] In other words, an individualised model of disability is applied to people with learning difficulties.

(Chappell et al., 2001, page 46)

Put simply, the argument made by Chappell et al. highlights the fact that the social model of disability still has some way to go. That is to say, although some groups or communities have adopted it, it has yet to be adopted by others. Thus, while some groups have begun to change how they think, write and speak about disabilities or learning difficulties, others have not.

Constructing discourses of disability

The ways in which people talk about disability in general, and learners with disabilities in particular, have changed considerably over recent years. Broader changes in social attitudes towards people with disabilities, spurred on and reinforced by successive pieces of government legislation, have helped start to create a quite different set of social attitudes towards people with disabilities. This is not to say that discrimination is a thing of the past, unfortunately. Nonetheless, opportunities for learners with disabilities are significantly greater than was the case even 20 years ago. And these changes in attitude can also be seen at work in how we, both as a society at large and also as teachers and trainers, talk about disability.

Changing discourses: from 'wheelchair-bound' to 'wheelchair user'

Perhaps the most conspicuous change in discourse around disability can be found in the actual word or words that are used when referring to disabilities. This can indeed be confusing, even embarrassing, for teachers and trainers. New words or expressions can take some time to become common parlance, while other expressions come and go more quickly. Sometimes, advocacy groups who represent particular communities of people with disabilities promote certain forms of expression: for example, whether to refer to a learner who is 'deaf' (with a small 'd') or 'Deaf' (with a capital 'd'); or whether to refer to a learner who is 'disabled' or 'differently abled'. Just as it is important not to stereotype learners with disabilities and assume that they are all 'the same' and therefore 'need' the same kinds of learning support, so it is also important to remember that among people with disabilities there are plenty of debates about how they should represent or construct themselves.

Other changes of terminology are perhaps less controversial. The contrasting examples given above, 'wheelchair-bound' and 'wheelchair user', are a case in point. The former was once a commonly used term, but now has almost completely disappeared. The term 'wheelchair-bound' is an example of a medical or deficit model of disability in action: the word 'bound' implies that the person using the wheelchair is somehow stuck or trapped, lacking the 'freedom' to stand up and do something. The term 'wheelchair user' shows a social model of disability at work: the person using the wheelchair simply happens to use a wheelchair, but that in itself is not a problem. What is important, when referring to disability, is that we, as teachers and trainers, address our learners in such a way that any disability is referred to without using language that is pejorative, diminishing or negative, and that people without disabilities are never referred to as 'normal'. Some other examples of appropriate terminology are:

- a person who is blind or partially sighted, not 'visually handicapped';
- a person with epilepsy, not 'an epileptic';
- a person with mental health difficulties, not 'mentally ill';
- a person with a disability, not 'a disabled person'.

But at the same time, it is important to keep a sense of perspective. There is nothing offensive about using expressions such as 'see you later' or 'do you see what I mean' when talking to a group of students that includes one student who is blind. Nor is there anything offensive about saying to a group of students that you are going to 'brainstorm' some ideas and write them on the board at the front of the room.

Changing discourses: from 'integration' to 'inclusion'

The language used by teachers in the classroom or workshop is a good example of how changing attitudes are reflected in the ways that we talk. A second good example can be found in the words used by government in policy documents, or by academics in books (such as this one!). One of the most conspicuous examples of changes in terminology that reflect changes in attitudes and practice is in the adoption of the term 'inclusion', which has replaced 'integration' as a central characteristic of responses to students with disabilities.

During our discussion of the Warnock Report (1978) earlier in this chapter, we highlighted that one of its aims was to encourage the integration of students with disabilities within mainstream institutional settings. It has been argued that there were three kinds of integration envisaged, which can be interpreted as operating on a sliding scale:

- Locational integration: when SEN students would be at the same location as 'mainstream' students, but would be housed in either a separate building or a separate classroom;
- Social integration: when SEN students would again be in separate accommodation for teaching, but would share social spaces with the rest of the student group (such as during lunchtimes, breaks and the like);
- Functional integration: when SEN students would spend either part or all of their time studying alongside the 'mainstream' students, sharing classrooms, staff and curricula.

There has been considerable discussion about the Warnock Report, fuelled in no small part by Mary Warnock herself in a pamphlet published in 2005 titled *Special Educational Needs: a new look*, in which she acknowledged, and in some cases endorsed, critiques of the very concept of 'special educational needs' and the balance between 'mainstream' and 'special' education. Notwithstanding these more recent controversies, however, it is undeniably the case that the original Warnock Report established a particular *discourse* around SEN and SEN provision for many years. More recently, the concept of inclusion has come to replace integration as the 'catch-all' term that is used to describe broad governmental and institutional approaches to educational provision:

> *Integration was the term first introduced in the 1978 Warnock Report. It was referring to the concept of integrating children with SEN into a common educational framework. The concept has since progressed to the inclusion of all children to reflect the idea that it is not for SEN children to be somehow fitted in or integrated into the mainstream but that education as a whole should be fully inclusive of all children.*
>
> (House of Commons Education and Skills Committee, 2006, page 22)

Although the focus of this chapter is quite narrow, it is important to remember that the shift from integration to inclusion requires us to consider not only the education of students with disabilities or learning difficulties, but also the education of other students who, for whatever reason, come from social or ethnic groups that have in the past been under-represented, even ill-served, by education providers (as established by the deliberately far-ranging definition of inclusive practice that we outlined in the introduction). But whether we talk about inclusive practice in terms of ensuring that formal education and training opportunities are able to be adapted to meet the needs of single parents (for example through the provision of crèche facilities at a subsidised rate for students), or are able to meet the needs of students with SEN (for example through the provision of assistive computer technology), the same concept of inclusion applies. By this, we mean to stress that rather than treat students with disabilities as a 'separate' group who need to be integrated into 'mainstream' provision, the focus shifts to the institution that is required to provide educational facilities or opportunities to anyone who, allowing for reasonable adjustments, is able to participate. At the same time, we are aware of the fact that for all kinds of reasons, access to education and training for students with disabilities (or, indeed, for other students who exhibit 'dimensions of difference') continues to be problematic.

Constructing responses to disability

As social attitudes towards disability have changed, so have the ways in which we, as teachers and trainers, respond to disability in both our professional and private lives. It is now not uncommon for images of people with disabilities to appear in the mainstream media, on film or in print, in stark contrast to the institutionalisation of people with disabilities that was prevalent only a few decades ago. As such, it seems right to say that our professional responses to students with disabilities are in part shaped or mediated by our broader attitudes towards disability, which in turn are shaped by these broader changes in social attitude, just as attitudes towards black and minority ethnic populations, or the role of women in society, have changed. Changes in societal attitudes do not happen in a vacuum, however: they are accompanied and encouraged by advocacy groups (such as the Alliance for Inclusive Education or the British Deaf Association), and enacted through government legislation. As such, all of these factors can be seen as having impacted on the ways in which we, both as a profession and as members of a wider society, respond to disability.

REFLECTIVE TASK

Responses to disability

Take a few moments to consider how you might respond, or have responded, to disabled students in your own professional practice. What kinds of support mechanisms or advice and guidance systems are there in your place of employment? If a student told you that they had a disability, would you know who to talk to within your college to help that student get the support that they need? If you are a full-time PGCE/CertEd student, you can talk to your mentor about the kinds of facilities that are available for students with disabilities. Do you in fact have a disability or learning difficulty? If so, how effectively do you think that, during your education history, institutions have responded to your needs?

In the introduction to this book, we referred to the fact that it is not uncommon for teachers in further or adult education to be the first 'port of call' for students with learning difficulties or disabilities. By this we meant to draw attention to the role played by teachers and trainers in diagnosing and, in the first instance, reacting to the differential needs that such students bring to the classroom or workshop. Some disabilities are straightforwardly conspicuous, but others are not. And although there are a number of different diagnostic assessment mechanisms that potential or new students can access, it remains the case that a student is not required to disclose a disability if she or he does not wish to do so. In our experience, this can cause some level of confusion among teacher-training students. Nonetheless, it is important to remember that it is the right of the individual to declare their disability, should they choose to do so. We would argue that it is in the best interests of students to do so, so that they can receive proper support, access to the appropriate diagnostic assessments, and advice about any additional support (including funding) that they might be entitled to. And it is also important to remember that should a student disclose a disability to you as their module tutor or class leader, they have notified *the institution as a whole* as far as the law is concerned. Consequently, if that student feels that they have been treated in a discriminatory manner, then the institution – not the individual tutor – is at fault. Therefore, if a student were to declare a disability, it is very important for you to inform other relevant staff members at once. Colleges and adult education providers usually have named contacts such as disability officers, or learning support managers, who will almost always be more informed about disability issues than the teaching staff as a whole.

RESEARCH FOCUS RESEARCH FOCUS **RESEARCH FOCUS** RESEARCH FOCUS **RESEARCH FOCUS**

Students with disabilities in mainstream FE

In a research paper published in 2006, Anne-Marie Wright explored the experiences of students with learning difficulties who were attending mainstream FE colleges. Drawing on her own experiences as a lecturer, on a small number of interviews carried out with students and on a review of a number of relevant policy documents and pieces of prior research, Wright argued that although FE colleges promised much, the reality of the provision that they offered for students with learning difficulties was marginal rather than mainstream, sustaining a culture of dependency rather than allowing students to access the mainstream vocational curriculum as a first step to employment. In her conclusion, she wrote:

If further education is serious about continuing to provide an inclusive experience for students with severe learning difficulties by providing courses which respond effectively to their real needs, it must commit not only to providing learning which meets the needs and aspirations of learners, but it must also work once again to strengthen partnerships with providers of employment and other services. Rather than allowing students to revisit comfortable, unchallenging experiences, colleges need to re-focus and see the bigger, longer-term picture. Imagine an 'access' course which did not provide careers guidance or support for applications for places in higher education and which did not link with a local university. Why should there be a difference for learners with severe difficulties?

(Wright, 2006, page 38)

While acknowledging the excellent work that many FE teachers and managers do to support SEN students, Wright nonetheless turns a spotlight on some aspects of provision that clearly need to be revised. If we accept that one of the main functions of the FE sector is to deliver a curriculum that allows the young people who go through it to access employment, apprenticeships or further training, then it seems right to say that if we are indeed trying to offer an *inclusive curriculum* (to which we shall return in Chapter 7), then that curriculum needs not only to be open to all students – whether they have a disability or learning difficulty, or not – but needs also to function in the same way for all students. That is to say, if the curriculum is indeed all about employability, then it needs to be employability for all. If the curriculum is all about opening up new opportunities for people, then it needs to do so for everyone who wishes to access it. If not only tutors but also colleges as institutions are to adopt a social model of disability, then our responses towards disability need to be about more than building ramps, installing lifts and providing learning support (although in the economic and political climate at the time we are writing this book, many learning support workers within the FE sector are facing redundancy). They need to be about viewing the student as a person, an individual with individual talents, motivations, skills and possibilities.

Conclusion

Medical, political and social attitudes to disability have changed profoundly during the last century. And at the same time, political and social attitudes to the provision of education and training have changed. Many at the turn of the twentieth century viewed the participation of women in higher education with equal parts of hostility and disbelief, and yet at the time of writing this book there are more women than men studying in universities in the UK. Students with disabilities and learning difficulties have yet to make such a significant level of progress, however. But their place in mainstream education is improving. And we would argue that it is through the wider adoption of a social rather than medical model of disability that profound attitudinal change can be brought about.

A SUMMARY OF **KEY POINTS**

In this chapter, we have looked at the following key points:

> **the basis of medical and social models of disability;**

> **the ways in which medical and social models have informed or influenced the attitudes and practices of teachers in the Lifelong Learning sector;**

> **social and political definitions and constructions of disability and SEN.**

A critical and thorough exploration of changing attitudes towards disability in general, and towards the place of people with disabilities within educational systems in particular, could easily fill a book twice the size of this one, and for those PGCE/CertEd students who have either the time or the inclination, further reading is recommended. Although this discussion has of necessity been relatively brief, we believe that through developing a more reflective and critical understanding of the ways in which people with disabilities have been seen and see themselves, our professional practice, as teachers and trainers, can become more responsive to their needs.

REFERENCES AND FURTHER READING REFERENCES AND FURTHER READING

Books

Curtis, W and Pettigrew, A (2010) *Education Studies: reflective reader*. Exeter: Learning Matters.

Warnock, M (2005) *Special Educational Needs: a new look*. London: Philosophy of Education Society.

Wright, A-M, Abdi-Jama, S, Colquhoun, S, Speare, J and Partridge, T (2006) *FE Lecturer's Guide to Diversity and Inclusion*. London: Continuum.

Journal articles

Chappell, A, Goodley, D and Lawthom, R (2001) Making connections: the relevance of the social model of disability for people with learning difficulties. *British Journal of Learning Disabilities*, 29(1): 45–50.

Wright, A-M (2006) Provision for students with learning difficulties in general colleges of further education – have we been going round in circles? *British Journal of Special Education*, 33(1): 33–39.

Government publications

House of Commons Educational and Skills Committee (2006) *Special Educational Needs*. London: The Stationery Office Limited.

3
Planning for specific learning difficulties and/or disabilities

By the end of this chapter you should:

- have an increasing understanding of the characteristics of the more commonly seen specific learning difficulties;
- develop your own philosophical position about specific learning difficulties and use this to help inform your teaching and learning practices;
- have a developing understanding of how you can plan your sessions to enable those with specific learning difficulties, as well as other learners, to participate fully in sessions and how ongoing evaluation of your practice can help you to plan better for the future needs of your learners;
- have a developing understanding of the theoretical underpinning to the diagnosis of specific learning difficulties.

Professional Standards

This chapter relates to the following Professional Standards:

Professional Values:

AS 1 Learners, their progress and development, their learning goals and aspirations and the experience they bring to their learning.

AS 3 Equality, diversity and inclusion in relation to learners, the workforce and the community.

Professional Knowledge and Understanding:

AK 3.1 Issues of equality, diversity and inclusion.

DK 1.1 How to plan appropriate, effective, coherent and inclusive learning programmes that promote equality and engage with diversity.

Professional Practice:

AP3.1 Apply principles to evaluate and develop own practice in promoting equality and inclusive learning and engaging with diversity.

BP 5.2 Select, develop and evaluate resources to ensure they are inclusive, promote equality and engage with diversity.

Introduction

In this chapter some of the more common hidden disabilities are explored. When planning this chapter we felt that time should be spent exploring some of the harder-to-detect learning difficulties and/or disabilities, as tutors have to be prepared to plan learning to meet the needs of these learners as well as those with the more easily identifiable learning difficulties seen in Lifelong Learning sector provision. Dyslexia, and to a lesser extent dyscalculia and dyspraxia, are often encountered in the Lifelong Learning sector, but not always readily understood and accommodated. The number of learners whose dyslexia (for example) is only diagnosed for the first time when arriving within the Lifelong Learning sector is considerable. Specialist awards and qualifications for staff exist, but are only usually undertaken by a minority of teachers or support workers who specialise in SEN. Many teachers in further education encounter these behaviours among their students but are rarely formally trained in managing them. Therefore this chapter provides an accessible account for the psychology of such behaviours, together with practical strategies for tutors to use to enable all to access the curriculum.

Introducing specific learning difficulties

The term 'specific learning difficulties' (SpLDs) is an umbrella term that encompasses a range of specific disorders of learning such as dyslexia, dyspraxia and dyscalculia. The term 'specific' indicates that there is a clearly identifiable and discrete area of learning that is affected, rather than progress in learning in general, as with some other more general learning difficulties and/or disabilities. The names of these disorders help to identify the specific areas of learning affected. If we break the names of these difficulties down we can gain some idea, but before we do so we need to understand that all of the words that describe these learning difficulties are Ancient Greek in origin. If we take the prefix 'dys' this literally means 'difficulty with', and when placed before 'lexia' meaning words, 'difficulty with words'; 'praxia' is related to praxis, or physical performance, movement in some way, hence 'difficulty with movement and co-ordination'; and 'calculia' relates to numbers, hence 'difficulty with numbers'.

One of the key issues in identifying if a learner in your classroom has a specific learning difficulty is that these types of difficulties are 'hidden' disabilities, that is, they have no clearly identifiable physical characteristics in comparison to some learning difficulties and/or disabilities, such as Down's Syndrome. To the untrained eye, the learner can often be seen to be fully participating in learning. More often than not, it's not until the first piece of work is submitted for marking that concerns about the learner might be raised. Consider the following case study:

CASE STUDY 1

Colin is teaching A Level History in the Sixth Form Centre of an FE college. It is a fairly large class of learners, 22 in total. The first assignment to be submitted by the learners is to be fairly brief, a one thousand word critical summary of the French Revolution, its causes, who was involved, the political drivers and so forth. This subject has been discussed in class at great length, with historical documentaries and various other TV programmes watched as a vehicle to focus the discussions. Ray, a very keen student, has shown excellent understanding of the programmes used and demonstrated this during discussions in the classroom. He was very vocal about his opinions, contributing very effectively to group discussions and generally helping others in the group to evaluate their own viewpoint. Colin was looking forward to reading Ray's first piece of written work. On doing so he was shocked. The work was scruffy, letters were badly formed and it was littered with spelling errors and crossings out. The writing was disorganised and disjointed; it had ideas abandoned halfway through, then returned to some time later, making the discussion and evaluation of the work difficult, if not impossible to follow at times. There was also evidence of reading and copying problems, with references from books being copied down incorrectly. The work also showed patches of true insight and understanding, which was reflective of Ray's classroom participation, but which were almost lost because of the broader problems with the work. What could be the explanation behind this apparent discrepancy between Ray's oral and written ability? What was Colin to feed back to Ray about the work?

What has been described above can be seen to be a typical example of an adult learner with dyslexic and potentially dyspraxic tendencies. The teaching methods utilised by the teacher, of watching TV programmes and discussion and debate, have enabled Ray to participate in the lessons fully and as such are an example of inclusive practice. But at the same time they have masked Ray's problems with reading, writing and organisational skills.

What Ray has demonstrated is an aspect of the *spiky profile* that can be seen in learners with a specific learning difficulty, that is, performing as expected in some areas but not in others. Within the medical model of dyslexia (Shaywitz, 1998) it is still commonly believed that to have a 'proper' diagnosis of dyslexia there has to be a marked discrepancy between IQ and reading and writing ability, or, in other words, an unexpected difficulty with the development of reading and writing skills when the apparent intelligence to develop these skills is in place. This has been rejected in recent years by practitioners and advocates of dyslexia who insist that learners with lower intelligence can also show the patterns and characteristics associated with this particular learning difficulty. Let's look at this more closely.

Specific learning difficulties in context

According to The British Dyslexia Association (BDA), it is estimated that around 10% of the population have dyslexia, and that many of these individuals also have characteristics of dyspraxia. This means that in any one classroom situation there may be up to three learners with dyslexia/dyspraxia, which is either diagnosed or undiagnosed. Therefore the situation depicted in the above case study, or something similar, is a phenomenon you are likely to come across more than once in your career as a teacher or trainer and as such it is beneficial to know something about the causes of these difficulties and what we as teachers can do, at a practical level, to assist our learners by making the learning and assessment process as inclusive as possible.

What also makes dealing with these hidden learning difficulties problematic is that the identification of them is still subject to much debate and even today there are people who doubt the very existence of dyslexia or dyspraxia. This confusion isn't helped by the numerous conflicting theoretical standpoints developed by different groups who have different perspectives on what dyslexia is and how it is defined. Some groups are advocates of dyslexia, such as the BDA, some are practitioners who are working in the field to support learners with these difficulties, such as Cynthia Klein, and some are scholars such as Snowling, Frith and Shaywitz who work within the medical model of dyslexia. All have different views about the condition and its cause, none of which fully explains all the difficulties associated with this particular learning difficulty (NRDC, 2004). This is further compounded by the disorder itself, as no learner ever follows the exact same pattern of characteristics, though there is a pattern of identifiable problems or key 'at risk' factors (Fawcett and Nicolson, 1998) that can indicate if a person may have dyslexia.

As tutors there are some more obvious characteristics of dyslexia, dyspraxia and dyscalculia we need to be aware of in order to have a better chance of identifying learners in a learning group that may have a learning difficulty. Although according to the International Dyslexia Association dyscalculia in its 'classic' form only affects 4% of the population, and you are therefore less likely to have a person with dyscalculia in your classroom, it is still useful to know some of the characteristics and difficulties to look out for. This is particularly important as, in law, tutors are expected to accommodate the needs of learners and make 'reasonable adjustments' to their practices as outlined in the Disability Discrimination Act Part 4 (2003), now superseded by the 2010 Equality Act, to ensure that learners can access learning as fully as possible.

We will now spend some time exploring specific learning difficulties in some detail, beginning with definitions of dyslexia, dyspraxia and dyscalculia as understood from both the medical and educational models. We will then go on to look at these difficulties using the social model of disability, and summarise some of the key defining factors of each.

The BDA (dyslexia), the Dyspraxia Foundation (dyspraxia) and the International Dyslexia Association (dyscalculia) use the medical/educational model to describe the specific learning difficulties. All of these definitions are based on a deficit model which rests on the assumption that something is wrong with the individual learner at a functional/biological level which then manifests itself in the difficulties we observe in the classroom.

Dyslexia

Dyslexia can be summarised as a life-long, usually genetic, inherited condition affecting around 10% of the population regardless of race, background and ability, which occurs independently of intelligence. It is a difficulty in information processing. For example, people with dyslexia may have difficulty processing and remembering information they see and hear and this can affect learning and the acquisition of literacy skills. It is also often accompanied by difficulties with spatial and temporal awareness, deficits in short-term memory, poor sequencing skills, poor organisational skills and difficulties settling on a 'dominant' side (left- or right-handed), leading to confused laterality. Dyslexia is one of a family of SpLDs. It often co-occurs with related conditions, such as dyspraxia, dyscalculia and attention deficit disorder (as we shall discuss later in this chapter). It varies from person to person and no two people will have the same set of strengths and weaknesses. Individuals with dyslexia can also suffer from low self-esteem and anxiety, perhaps linked to being told they are 'different' or due to ongoing and repeated failure in learning. People with dyslexia often have strong visual, creative and problem-solving skills and are prominent among entrepreneurs, inventors, architects, engineers and in the arts and entertainment world.

Dyspraxia

Learners with dyspraxia may have spatial awareness difficulties. For example, they may find it difficult to judge distances and heights. They may have difficulties with the co-ordination of gross and fine motor skills leading to apparent clumsiness and untidy, unintelligible handwriting respectively. They may have difficulty with word pronunciation; have poor concentration skills and deficits in their short-term memory. Also often seen are difficulties with sequencing tasks and consequently with the organisation of thoughts and of themselves, often finding it difficult to organise their writing and meet deadlines for assignments, which they may forget about. They can also find it extremely stressful being in large group situations, become easily anxious and depressed.

Dyscalculia

Dyscalculia can be defined as a dysfunction in the reception, comprehension or production of quantitative (numerical and/or statistical) and spatial information. It is a learning difficulty in conceptualising numbers, number relationships, outcomes of numerical operations and estimation. These specific problems in number manipulation are often accompanied by difficulties with temporal and spatial awareness, such as time-keeping, lack of space awareness (for example, distances) and problems with laterality and direction, following instructions (for example, sequential directions) and general sequencing.

Dyslexia, dyspraxia and dyscalculia: is there a link?

Research shows that there is a degree of overlap between some of the characteristics and related problems in learning of dyslexia and dyspraxia, though dyslexia is primarily a difficulty with reading and writing and dyspraxia an impairment of the organisation of movement. There are other common characteristics of both of these learning difficulties, such as poor organisational skills, short-term memory problems and difficulties with spatial awareness. According to the International Dyslexia Association there is no *direct link* between dyslexia and dyscalculia, and in fact it is not uncommon for people with dyslexia to have some problems with the organisation and manipulation of numbers and number relationships. This is unsurprising when we consider that mathematics is essentially language-based, as understanding the language of mathematics is essential to being able to solve mathematical problems, as is the ability to hold and manipulate information in the short-term memory (STM). STM has a much-reduced capacity in people with dyslexia. According to Lee (2002), the average 'chunk' of information held in STM for a person without impaired STM is 6–9 pieces, whereas for a person with impaired STM it is an average of 3–5. To demonstrate this we can look at one of the tests that educational psychologists use to measure STM capacity, called a Digit Span test. This test measures the chunks of information (in this case number sequences delivered in a very specific way) that can be retained in the STM for a measured period of time. This is a standardised test, which has demonstrated over time that learners with dyslexia can often only retain on average between 3 and 5 numbers but that a respondent without impaired STM capacity would normally be able to retain an average of between 6 and 9 numbers. The capacity of the STM affects the ability to organise and sequence information. Not only is this capacity vital for learning in general, it is also essential for the solution of mathematical problems. In this instance we can see how the dyslexic condition will have a direct impact on mathematical ability. The International Dyslexia Association (October 2010, accessed online) suggests that the key contrasting feature between dyslexia and dyscalculia is that people with dyscalculia do not have a language-based problem, but a specific problem with the taking in of, comprehension and/or production of quantitative and spatial information.

In summary, although there are definite areas of overlap with some skill deficits, because of the individuality and variability of the different characteristics of the conditions from individual to individual, it is impossible to come up with a definitive 'checklist'. Therefore, the following table should not be taken as being exhaustive or even definitive, but as a general indicator of the types of areas of specific difficulty you may observe in your learners.

Characteristic	Dyslexia	Dyspraxia	Dyscalculia
Deficits in phonological awareness	✓	✗	✗
Difficulties in acquiring fluent reading skills	✓	✓	✗
Difficulties with writing and spelling	✓	✓	✗
Difficulty with number manipulation and calculation	✓	✓	✓
Slow information processing	✓	✓	✓
Deficits in short-term memory	✓	✓	✓
Difficulties with laterality	✓	✓	✓
Poor spatial awareness	✓	✓	✓
Poor temporal awareness	✓	✓	✓
Poor organisational skills	✓	✓	✓
Poor sequencing skills	✓	✓	✓
Occurs across the range of intellectual abilities	✓	✓	✓
It is best thought of as a continuum, not a distinct category, and there are no clear cut-off points	✓	✓	x

REFLECTIVE TASK

Think about the information you have just read about the characteristics of the SpLDs outlined above. Are there any learners in any of your learning groups that come to mind when reading the definitions? Have you any learners with formal diagnosis of a SpLD, and if so, can you now relate any aspects of the definitions to their performance in learning and assessment tasks?

Testing for SpLDs, particularly dyslexia

There are many people who struggle to obtain the basic skills of reading, writing and numeracy to a level that may enable them to function in society and the world of work. This is often more likely to be for reasons that are not related to having a specific impairment such as dyslexia, dyspraxia or dyscalculia. One of the current issues we must be aware of as teachers and trainers is over-diagnosis, or more worryingly self-diagnosis, of a specific learning difficulty, particularly dyslexia. There is a range of tests that are becoming more freely available. Some are screening tests, some of which are considered to be relatively reliable, such as the Dyslexia Adult Screening Test (Fawcett and Nicolson, 1998) which is carried out by trained practitioners. Other internet screening tests are freely available, generally of the tick-box type and designed by advocates and sometimes practitioner groups. There are some diagnostic tests, one of the most commonly used by practitioners being the Diagnostic Assessment Materials for Dyslexia box (2002, DfES) which is free and part of the Skills for Life range of materials. There are also full psychological assessments which use standardised tests such as the Digit Span test, the Wechsler Adult Intelligence Scale (WAIS) and the Wide Range Achievement Test (WRAT). Full psychological assessments are normally carried out by educational psychologists, but some practitioners, when following approved programmes of training, can also carry out assessments that are recognised by awarding bodies and enable them to complete diagnostic assessments and apply for special concessions for students sitting exams, such as extra time or an amanuensis.

PRACTICAL TASK PRACTICAL TASK PRACTICAL TASK PRACTICAL TASK PRACTICAL TASK

Search the web to find out as much as you can about the assessment of dyslexia. See what types of 'tests' are available: screening, diagnostic, full psychological and such like. If a learner came to you with the results from these tests, you should be able to interpret what they mean or be able to discuss them (with the learner's permission) with the SENCO in the college or school. You need to have a rough idea about a) what they test and what the results mean; b) how valid and reliable they are; and c) any implications for your teaching practice and assessment of learning, for example, a learner with a full diagnosis by a recognised dyslexia specialist may be entitled, in an exam, to a reader, an amanuensis and extra time. If this is the case, you will need to liaise with the appropriate person in your organisation who can make the appropriate arrangements.

When you have completed the above, spend some time reflecting on what you have discovered by completing the following reflective task.

REFLECTIVE TASK

How useful do you think online dyslexia tests are? Are they dangerous? What precedents do they set for those with difficulties in reading and writing? Is there a danger of over-diagnosis by amateurs or advocates and what might this mean to you as a practitioner? What do you need to be aware of in terms of learners who come to you and say they've been assessed as having dyslexia?

Dyslexia and the social model of disability

We have spent some time looking at the medical/educational models of dyslexia. However, it is equally important to spend some time looking at SpLDs using the social model of disability as discussed in the preceding chapter. This differs fundamentally from the medical model or 'deficit or dysfunction' model espoused by many (Morton, 2004; Nicholson and Fawcett, 1994; Olson, 2002; Snowling, 2000; Stein and Talcott, 1999), as it considers and defines SpLDs as a social rather than as an individual problem and states that the barriers that prevent people moving through education, employment and life are caused by the social and cultural structures that are built around the individual rather than based on any learning difficulties that the individual may have. Therefore, the barriers to educational progression and/or employment that individuals with SpLDs may encounter can be seen as a result of more wider structural and institutional inequalities that create barriers to learning and gaining employment, rather than the individual's specific problems, in whatever area, creating the barrier (Macdonald, 2009).

If we use an approach to planning learning and teaching for learners with SpLDs which considers aspects of the models we have discussed, we are more likely to be able to meet the needs of the learners and provide them with the best possible opportunities to meet their potential. We would suggest use of the social model, which looks at the environment around the learner and at what strategies can be implemented to help the learner overcome the barriers and thus promote inclusion, rather than the medical or deficit model, which focuses on the underlying issues in the learners themselves.

However, as tutors and trainers it is important that we have some understanding of the theoretical background to the underlying causes, so that we understand some of the reasons for the difficulties our learners face.

THEORY FOCUS **THEORY** FOCUS **THEORY** FOCUS **THEORY** FOCUS **THEORY** FOCUS

Many practitioners and theorists discuss dyslexia as being a deficit in the ability to process language due to three parts of the brain not functioning as they should do.

Lee (2002) summarises these theories well. The language areas in the brain are located in the left hemisphere, which is the centre for language processing. Much research has been done in this area, which has concluded that the language areas in the dyslexic brain do not function in language processing as they should, leading to poor and inaccurate phonological processing and phonological awareness (or the ability to apply sounds to letters and letter combinations). This links directly to a delay in the development of reading and spelling skills.

The second part of the brain which seems not to be functioning as it should in learners with dyslexia and dyspraxia (and possibly dyscalculia) is the cerebellum, or little brain. The cerebellum is said to be significantly less active in those identified as having SpLDs. This is important because as knowledge of the role of the cerebellum has grown, so has the understanding of its importance in learning. It was once thought that the cerebellum's only function was in motor co-ordination, but more recent research has demonstrated it has a major role in cognition and developing skill automaticity. Fawcett and Nicholson (1998) suggest that the cerebellum is directly linked to the language areas in the brain and has a major function in smoothing cortical data. If the cerebellum is not working correctly, this might result in the wrong 'decision' being made by the brain cortex, for example, the wrong word being read or faulty sound processing in applying phonological approaches to reading. An inactive cerebellum also has an impact on becoming automatic in learning a new skill. When we are learning a new skill it takes up our short-term memory, but as we become automatic in that skill we use less short-term memory as automaticity takes over. This is a very important aspect of learning. In learners with SpLDs it takes much longer to become automatic at a skill, so the short-term memory is not being freed up as quickly as it should be, leading to short-term memory overload and slow skill automaticity development. This could explain why some dyslexic learners become proficient readers as adults, as they have at last got some automaticity in reading but it has taken much longer than normally expected to acquire the skill.

Consider the following case study. It demonstrates how an individual mastering an everyday task moves from novice (mechanical) to expert (automatic).

CASE STUDY 2

Dawn is an experienced driver. She has been watching a driving school programme on the TV and is reflecting upon how much her driving has changed from her very first lesson to becoming a competent driver. She recalls how much effort and concentration it took to learn the new skills. How all she could concentrate on was the car and its operation, for example checking the mirror, putting the car into gear, driving, changing gear, braking and trying to observe all that was happening around her. Now she is an experienced driver she can't believe how different the experience is. Now when she is driving she thinks about her upcoming day at work, plans the evening meal and can arrive at work and find that she hardly remembers driving the car or any of the journey at all. What has changed?

The above case study is an example of how becoming automatic at a skill 'frees up' short-term memory. While learning to drive, the mechanics of operating the car had all of Dawn's attention and her short-term memory was full to capacity. As she became a more skilled driver (or moving to automaticity) less of her short-term capacity was needed, thus freeing it up to think about other things. When she became fully automatic in her driving, she used virtually no short-term memory capacity at all, hence not remembering the process of moving the car from one destination to another, just leaving and arriving.

We will now consider one more area of theory.

THEORY FOCUS **THEORY** FOCUS **THEORY** FOCUS **THEORY** FOCUS **THEORY** FOCUS

The final area to look at is temporal and visual processing. Tallal (1976) discovered that learners with dyslexia are not as quick at picking up rapidly flowing sounds and are generally slower at language processing. This means that in a classroom situation learners with this difficulty can lose track of what is being said and fall behind very easily. Lovegrove (1990) and Livingston (1991) identified that in learners with dyslexia the magnocells which control the efficiency and speed of visual, and some think auditory, processing have not developed properly and suggest that this is linked (though this is not proven) to some of the visual disturbances that some learners with dyslexia report, such as blurring and letters moving around on the page or running off the page, and the mechanical approaches to reading that some learners with poor phonological awareness (or phonic attack) demonstrate.

Finally, we need to consider the research that has been carried out that defines dyslexia as a learning style. A learning style is fundamentally the preferred way that learners like to learn, for example, some learners like to read quietly and make summary notes, some learners prefer group discussions, some like to watch and listen to TV programmes, and some are hands-on learners who learn best from practical activities. Many attempts have been made at categorising learning styles. Fleming (*VAK and VARK*, 2001) and Gardner (*Multiple Intelligences*, 1983) are two of the more commonly known ones, but not everyone agrees that learning preferences are a sound educational basis on which to develop our teaching and learning strategies (Coffield et al., 2004). This aside, the research of Krupsa and Klein (1995) urges us to consider learners with dyslexia as right-brained learners. They argue that dyslexic learners, perhaps because of the deficits in the language areas in the left hemisphere, tend to be right-brain dominant in their learning and/or thinking. Therefore, when planning our teaching we could consider how we utilise right-brain learning/thinking skills, which are contrasted here with left-brain thinking skills:

Left brain	Right brain
Logical	Random
Sequential	Intuitive
Rational	Holistic
Analytical	Synthesising
Objective	Subjective
Looks at parts	Looks at wholes

We have explored a variety of definitions and models of SpLDs but what strategies can we plan to use in our classroom practices to support learners with a SpLD?

Considerations and practical strategies for supporting learners with SpLDs

There are a number of considerations we need to make in order to plan effectively for learners with SpLDs. We will start by looking at some examples followed by some more general considerations and strategies/tips.

The following case studies focus on three learners who have different educational needs, are at different stages in their lives and who are attending programmes of study in different educational settings. They are intended to demonstrate learning situations which we as tutors and trainers in Lifelong Learning may come across and will hopefully be a useful tool for reflection on our own teaching practice.

CASE STUDY 3
Adult Education

Mark is 26, has dyslexia, and has a repeated history of schooling failure in learning to read and write. He left school with no qualifications in English. As an adult Mark's reading skills have developed, mostly as a result of him persisting in reading what he likes to read, i.e. reading for enjoyment. Mark is self-employed, as what started as a hobby for him, photography, has turned into a job. His business is growing, and he has found that his lack of writing skills is starting to hold him back. For example, he writes down names and phone numbers incorrectly and finds it difficult to complete the book-keeping requirements due to poor spelling and poor organisational skills. He approaches an adult learning centre which offers a range of programmes in literacy and numeracy which it says can be tailored to working practices. However, after six weeks Mark decides to leave the programme, as he finds himself on a structured, interventionist language programme which has taken him back to the basics of learning sound and letter combinations to improve his general spelling, which are not going to help him to develop the skills he needs to progress his business. He feels very let down and that he is back to square one and has wasted six weeks that he could have better spent.

CASE STUDY 4
Further Education

Stacey is studying A level media studies but is struggling to keep up in lectures. She doesn't have a diagnosed learning difficulty but finds that Barry, the lecturer, moves through the session very quickly, gives a lot of information orally and encourages the students to take copious amounts of notes. He uses the whiteboard a lot to make key points, but erases the information quickly. He does not provide copies of any materials he uses and uses predominantly didactic (chalk and talk) teaching approaches. Stacey finds that when she leaves the classroom and tries to read her notes, they are messy with lots of information missing and all in all of little use to her. Barry puts brief notes on the college VLE as a word-processed document. Stacey approaches him after one of these sessions as she is finding it impossible to keep up and is falling further and further behind. She explains the problems she is having and tells Barry that she is thinking of leaving the programme.

Case study 3: Responses

What Mark needed were strategies to help him learn to spell the types of words he needs for work and for taking down phone numbers and organising himself and his book-keeping. The centre should have built the following into a learning programme for Mark:

- a multi-sensory spelling programme (Lee, 2002) which would have provided a focused and structured way for Mark to learn the words he needed to spell;
- a skills development programme to include tips on how to get organised, e.g. using coloured paper, highlighter pens, etc.;
- recommending the use of assistive technology, e.g. a Dictaphone to record the names and numbers of clients rather than writing them down.

The programme the centre gave to Mark was interventionist and focused on the deficits that he had in general spelling, developing the skills that would occur in children with normal development before their teenage years. A noble ambition, but for Mark it failed to address the development of the skills he needed to get him past the barriers that were holding him back in his employment, which as a 26-year-old adult were his priorities.

Case study 4: Responses

Stacey may have an undiagnosed SpLD which means that her ability to keep up with what's happening in the classroom is severely impeded. She has approached her lecturer for help. What should he do and what should Stacey expect?

- Barry needs to consider what reasonable adjustments he can make in his teaching to enable Stacey to take part fully in the session and to support her needs outside of this. If Barry does not do this he is in danger of falling foul of the Disability Discrimination Act (1995).
- Barry could make some simple changes to his sessions which might help. He might think of building in some different teaching and learning strategies that don't just rely on listening and note-taking; he might encourage Stacey to bring a Dictaphone into his sessions so she can record his lectures and play them back as many times and as she needs while making summary notes; he might provide Stacey with an outline of the session and the presentations he is going to use a week in advance to help her to prepare for the session; or he might make better use of the VLE. These are just some examples of strategies that might assist Stacey in being more included in the learning process, but Barry *must* do something if he is not to break the law.
- Barry needs to urge Stacey to access the available support services; she is likely to benefit greatly from specialist help and guidance. He might reflect on whether a formal diagnosis of any learning difficulty might be of any real use to Stacey at this point in her Lifelong Learning, but must leave that decision to the specialists and Stacey herself. Referring Stacey is the right thing to do.

The use of teaching assistants

Teaching assistants (TAs) can be invaluable when working with learners with SpLDs, particularly in a busy classroom where a tutor might not always be able to provide the level of support needed, for example, proof-reading work, helping to organise writing, making new learning as multi-sensory as possible and developing study skills strategies, explaining concepts and helping with assistive technology such as voice recognition software. This is discussed in more detail in Chapter 6. However, if the TA and tutor are to work together effectively to best support the needs of learners with SpLDs, spending time together planning the learning that is to take place is essential. This can be problematical if finance for human resources is limited.

CASE STUDY 5

The role of the TA

Robert is 16 and has dyspraxia. As a result of this he has not done well at school in academic subjects and has progressed into a foundation studies programme at a college of FE which teaches basic work skills, English and mathematics. He finds it difficult to organise himself to get to college, and is often late and can't remember where he is timetabled to be for a lot of the time. When in class he appears to be keeping up with his work, but when Mary, the tutor, checks she finds that his writing is often incomprehensible and Robert can't read what he has written, which then leads to frustration and bouts of aggressive behaviour. He finds it difficult to follow both oral and written instructions due to problems with his short-term memory and poor reading skills, so he finds it difficult to complete practical tasks when following sequential instructions. For example, in a retailing session the learners were putting together boxes to package goods, and Robert could not manage this on his own. Mary spent most of the session with him and as a result felt that she had neglected the other learners' needs. Mary is unsure what to do to progress Robert in his learning, so she turns to the college's disability adviser for advice. She is getting increasingly frustrated by Robert's lack of progress and is increasing worried as his behaviour is deteriorating.

Case study 5: Responses

Robert is in need of additional support in the classroom. A TA would seem to be the best solution as this would help Mary to meet Robert's learning needs, removing the worry that he is being left to his own devices while she works with the other members of the group. This would provide him with the help and support he needs to complete tasks and thus avoid the frustrations which seem to be leading to the behavioural problems he is developing. Mary should:

- spend time planning the session with a TA so that both are clear about what is to be completed and where the roles and responsibilities of each begin and end;
- ensure that the TA utilises her role fully by meeting with the disability co-ordinator to establish Robert's needs both inside and outside the classroom, e.g. meeting Robert before class so that he can be taken to the right classroom;
- meet regularly with the TA to discuss Robert's progress.

Tips and strategies to consider when planning sessions

- Make sure you have as much detail about the needs of the learners in your group as possible. This will help you to plan more effectively for any learners with identified learning difficulties and/or disabilities.
- Build differentiated activities into your planning. Think about how individuals learn and how you can meet these needs in your planning, e.g. a learner with dyspraxia may be slower at completing a task, so differentiate by speed or extension for those that are quicker.
- Plan to use a variety of teaching and learning techniques/activities that encourage right- as well as left-brain learning. Use models, images and videos to provide solutions and get the learners to work out the answer. Don't just use Powerpoint, 'chalk and talk' and individual reading and writing tasks. The more creative you are in your teaching at the planning stage and the activities you provide for learners, the more inclusive you will be.

- Build time in to give you the opportunity to carry out some one-to-one support. Quite often learners with a SpLD find it difficult to take in information or instructions fully the first time round, so some one-to-one help can be extremely beneficial for them.
- Build in multi-sensory learning strategies where you can. This will encourage learners with dyslexia to use all the modalities of seeing, hearing, feeling and saying when they are completing learning activities (we will return to this in Chapter 6).
- As soon as possible you need to consider how you are going to make the assessment of learning as inclusive as possible. This might mean adapting something from a written assessment to an oral assessment, or if there are strict regulations about the type of assessment evidence the learner needs to produce you may need to consider exploring outside help, e.g. the use of an amanuensis.
- Build in the use of ICT in teaching sessions if possible and encourage the use of assistive software for learners as appropriate.
- Prepare resources as required by the learners. Some learners with dyslexia read better on coloured paper, or want presentations or handouts the week before to give them time to read and process the information before the taught session as this gives them a better chance of being prepared and for keeping up in class and participating fully.
- Make the session resources accessible outside of the classroom and make them as multi-sensory as possible, for example, using classroom capture (a video of your teaching session) and providing interactive activities. Copies of presentations and session notes made available via a VLE will help to make learning accessible at all times for all learners and will assist inclusive practices for those with SpLDs.
- Be aware that learners with SpLDs may have self-esteem and confidence issues, so plan to use lots of praise and positive feedback. Try to be sensitive, constructive and supportive when providing negative feedback if it's necessary, e.g. on failing an assessment task.
- Don't be afraid to ask for help. You are not meant to know everything! Some learners will benefit greatly from accessing specialist support which will help them to learn how they learn and may also provide them with strategies to help overcome some of their problems, such as organising work and developing short-term memory capacity, which can greatly help them in their more general learning. This will also provide opportunities for them to develop study skills strategies that might help them to cope more effectively in the normal classroom situation.
- Consider accessing some CPD if you feel that you need to know more about SpLDs in order for you to plan to meet the needs of your learners.
- Ask your learners and listen to the feedback they give about the completion of learning and assessment tasks and consider this in your future planning. Don't forget that as individuals with SpLDs move through adulthood they compensate to some extent by developing coping strategies as they learn about the ways in which they learn. They can pinpoint their strengths and weaknesses, and as tutors and trainers in Lifelong Learning we should be aware that their own evaluation of their strengths and weaknesses is just as important (and sometimes more so) than what screening or diagnostic assessments might tell us.

A SUMMARY OF **KEY POINTS**

In this chapter we have looked at the following key points:

> **what SpLDs are and what you might expect to encounter in your teaching practices in the Lifelong Learning sector;**

> **some of the theoretical underpinning for the diagnosis of SpLDs;**

> **some strategies and resources you can use when planning your teaching to meet the needs of learners with diagnosed and undiagnosed SpLDs or planning to be as inclusive in your teaching approaches as possible.**

In summary, be realistic about what you can do. Although we can look at removing many disabling barriers to learning for learners with SpLDs, the issue is broader than that. In a world which is ruled by the written word, and where the basic functions of language and mathematics can be seen to be fundamental to the educational, social and economic inclusion of individuals, we can conclude that learners with these hidden disabilities, even though they may have strengths in other areas, may still be more likely to be at a disadvantage when compared to other learners who do not have these specific problems in language and number-based learning.

REFERENCES AND FURTHER READING REFERENCES AND FURTHER READING

Books

Coffield, F, Moseley, D, Hall, E and Ecclestone, K (2004) *Learning Styles and Pedagogy in Post-16 Learning: a systematic and critical review.* London: Learning and Skills Network.

Fawcett, A J and Nicolson, R I (1994) *Dyslexian Children, Multidisciplinary Perspectives.* London: Harvester Wheatsheaf.

Fawcett, A and Nicolson, R I (1998) *The Dyslexia Adult Screening Test Manual.* Sheffield: The Psychological Corporation.

Fleming, N D (2001) *Teaching and Learning Styles: VARK Strategies.* Honolulu: Honolulu Community College.

Gardner, H (1993) *Frames of Mind: theory of multiple intelligences.* Tucson: Zephyr Press.

Klein, C (2003) *Diagnosing Dyslexia: A guide to the assessment of dyslexic adults.* London: Basic Skills Agency.

Krupska, M and Klein, C (1995) *Demystifying Dyslexia: raising awareness and developing support for dyslexic young people and adults:* London: London Language and Literacy Unit.

Lee, J (2002) *Making the Curriculum Work for Learners with Dyslexia.* London: Basic Skills Agency.

Morton, J (2004) *Understanding Developmental Disorders: A cognitive modelling approach.* Oxford: Blackwell.

Naidoo, S (1972) *Specific Dyslexia.* London: Pitman.

National Research and Development Centre for Adult Literacy and Numeracy (2004) *Developmental Dyslexia in Adults: a research review.* London: NRDC.

Reid, G (2003) *Dyslexia: a practitioner's handbook.* Chichester: Wiley Publications.

Snowling, M J (2000) *Dyslexia.* London: Blackwell.

Government publications

Department for Education and Skills (2004) *Understanding a Framework for Dyslexia.* Nottingham: Crown Publications.

The Rose Review (2009) *Independent Review of the Primary Curriculum.* Nottingham: Crown Publications.

Journal articles

Fawcett, A J and Nicolson, R I (1999) Dyslexia: the role of the cerebellum. *Dyslexia International Research and Practice*, 5: 155–77.

Livingston, M, Rosen, G D, Drislane, F and Galaburda, A (1991) Physiological evidence for a magnocellular deficit in developmental dyslexia. *Proceedings of the National Academy of Sciences*, 88: 7943–47.

Lovegrove, W J, Garzia, R P and Nicholson, S B (1990) Experimental evidence of a transient system deficit in reading ability. *Journal of the American Optometric Association*, 61: 137–46.

Macdonald, Stephen J (2009) Windows of reflection: conceptualizing dyslexia using the social model of disability. *Dyslexia*, 15: 347–62.

Olson, R K (2002) Dyslexia: nature and nurture. *Dyslexia*, 8: 143–59.

Scanlon, D and Lenz, K (2002) Intervention practices in adult literacy education for adults with learning disabilities. *Journal of Postsecondary Education and Disability*, 16(1): 32–49.

Shaywitz, Sally E (1998) Dyslexia. *New England Journal of Medicine*, 316: 1268–70.

Stein, J F and Talcott, J B (1999) Impaired neuronal timing in developmental dyslexia – the magnocellular hypothesis. *Dyslexia*, 5: 59–77.

Tallal, P (1976) Rapid auditory processing in normal and disordered language development. *Journal of Speech and Hearing Research*, 19: 561–71.

Websites

Disability Discrimination Act 1995 www.legislation.gov.uk/ukpga/1995/50/contents

Equality Act 2010 www.legislation.gov.uk/ukpga/2010/15/contents

International Dyslexia Association www.interdys.org

The British Dyslexia Association www.bdadyslexia.org.uk

Dyspraxia Foundation www.dyspraxiafoundation.org.uk

4
Managing the learning environment

By the end of this chapter you should:

- have a developing understanding of what constitutes challenging behaviour and some of the underlying causes of this;
- begin to develop an increasing awareness of the strategies that can be employed to manage challenging behaviour and promote inclusive learning;
- have a growing understanding of the implications of challenging behaviour on teaching and learning practices.

Professional Standards

This chapter relates to the following Professional Standards:

Professional Values:

AS 1 Learners, their progress and development, their learning goals and aspirations and the experience they bring to their learning.

AS 3 Equality, diversity and inclusion in relation to learners, the workforce and the community.

Professional Knowledge and Understanding:

AK 3.1 Issues of equality, diversity and inclusion.

BK 1.2 Ways to develop and manage behaviours which promote respect for and between others and create an equitable and inclusive learning environment.

Professional Practice:

B 1.2 Establish and maintain procedures with learners which promote and maintain appropriate behaviour, communication and respect for others, while challenging discriminatory behaviours and attitudes.

Introduction

There is no escaping the issue of behaviour when discussing inclusive practice. This is not to stereotype hard-to-reach students as always being disruptive, but nonetheless for many non-traditional and at-risk students, outward behaviour is often the first indication of another difficulty (this might be related to an undiagnosed disability, problems at home, difficulties with paying course fees – the scope is considerable). As teachers and trainers in the Lifelong Learning sector, we will often come across situations with learners both inside and outside of the classroom that we consider to be displaying challenging behaviour. This can be towards us as perceived figures of authority, towards classroom peers and sometimes towards the organisation itself. This chapter will explore some of the theoretical viewpoints about what challenging behaviour is and how this can be managed in learning and teaching situations. It will provide practical advice about spotting the signs that learners might need help but are unable or unwilling to express that need, and will also challenge the commonly held belief that challenging behaviour is always a negative thing. In short, this chapter is our contribution to the classroom management debate. We will begin by looking at what challenging behaviour is.

What is challenging behaviour?

Challenging behaviour is difficult to define. We might say that it is behaviour demonstrated by learners that is outside of what we might expect or plan for as teachers, or behaviours which do not always respond to normal classroom management strategies and which in some way disrupt the outcome we have planned for our teaching sessions. Challenging behaviour can show itself in many ways. Some of the more commonly seen, according to Wingert and Molitor (2009), are:

- being unprepared for classroom activities, for example not reading the pre-set texts required for the sessions;
- being inattentive, for example carrying out their own conversations or playing with mobile phones;
- being reluctant to participate in classes, for example sitting at the back of the class, not contributing to discussions, not completing tasks given to them;
- demonstrating hostile behaviour, for example overly aggressive actions and behaviour towards classmates and the tutor or trainer, slamming objects on the desk, using bad language, throwing things around the classroom, storming from the classroom;
- being argumentative: heated discussions may lead to hostile comments that are inappropriate to the learning situation, peers and the tutor or trainer.

Learners with learning difficulties and/or disabilities

Learners with learning difficulties and/or disabilities (LDD) may have additional barriers to learning and may demonstrate some or all of the challenging behaviours outlined previously if their needs are not being met. For example, a learner who struggles to read will not appreciate a relatively difficult reading and comprehension task. A learner who is partially sighted and needs enlarged papers to participate fully in lessons will not be able to participate unless the papers are provided. More generally, not having an awareness of the nature of the learners we have in our groups will make it difficult, if not impossible, for us to plan to meet their needs effectively. All these instances, and many more, can lead to bad experiences in the classroom for both the teacher or trainer, and the learner.

REFLECTIVE TASK

Sally is a full-time teacher-training student writing her learning journal and reflecting upon her experiences of working with some students to whom she is providing basic skills support. The learning group is a mixed group of learners from a range of vocational subject areas. Sally has been told that they need help with their literacy skills. As you read, think about the way Sally reports her experiences and those of the learners. Think about how you may be able to inform your own teaching and learning practices if you find yourself in a similar situation. Then read on to find out how Sally might tackle the issues that she raises in her journal.

It is my second week of providing support for the students, and I have to admit it isn't going well. There are four learners in total: two of the learners in the group are from motor vehicle studies I think, the other two are hairdressing students. David, one of the two motor vehicle students (I asked him and he confirmed that they were) seemed to be willing and tried to complete the work, but the other, Robert, refused to complete any of the reading or writing activities I had given to him. When I challenged him about this and pointed out that the other people in the group had attempted the task, he got up and left the classroom. He is going to be in serious bother when I report it back to his personal tutor. Well he can just have the task to do again next week. Jayne seemed to be a nice girl; it was her first week attending this week. She is doing hairdressing and I seem to remember being told that she had a learning difficulty of some type. I have another problem here: she was writing away, but when I read the work she produced (the students all had the same task to complete, they had to read sentences with words missing and using the context of the sentence select the right word from a choice of five words and write it in the gap), she had got them all wrong. It's as if she hadn't been able to read it at all. All I can remember when I looked at her was her working hard. I need to think about what I can do for her next week, refer to my Adult Literacy Core Curriculum for guidance. The other hairdressing student, James, seemed to want to spend all of his time chatting to the other students in the group and distracting them, which annoyed me. When I asked him to get on with his work he told me he had finished it, and when I checked he had, so he continued to try to distract the other two so I sent him away until next week. The other motor vehicle student asked to see me at the end, but I was rushing off to another class and told him to email me. He quickly told me that he might not be coming to any more sessions if he had any choice in the matter, that the work I had given him wasn't going to help him to pass his motor vehicle course so what was the point? I said the point was that he needed to learn to improve his reading and writing skills and would he go away and think about this and also attend the next session. He agreed to this. Then I had to race off and leave him. I really can't understand David and Robert! They surely must know they need to learn to read and write and why didn't Jayne tell me she couldn't read what I had given her and what am I to do with James? He found the task very easy to complete.

What is happening here? Sally finds herself in a position that many tutors of adult literacy encounter: the provision of learning support to a mixed group of learners of whom she knows little. What also isn't helping here is Sally's inexperience. She can clearly see that there are issues, but is unclear about the best way to deal with them. Where is Sally going wrong and how can she move this situation forward? Sally needs to begin by looking at the broader issues. She needs to evaluate the learners as a unit to see if there are any whole group strategies she can employ to manage the challenging behaviour she perceives to be happening. This might help to address the majority of the issues she has identified in her journal. Then she might consider looking at the individual learners, on a case-by-case basis, to see if there are any additional strategies she can put in place.

The whole group

Help with literacy skills
One of the key problems that literacy support tutors have to deal with when working with disparate groups of learners like this is a lack of information. Sally has been told that the learners need help with 'literacy skills' but has no idea about the levels of literacy the learners are functioning at, so has provided all of the learners with the same task. She needs to find out from the learners' personal tutors as much information as she can about the learners' levels of ability and what underlying learning difficulties any of the learners may have: just some very basic information, such as whether the learners are functioning at entry levels 1, 2 or 3, or level 1 or 2 in their literacy skills, or whether they have any identified LDDs. This will help Sally to promote inclusion in learning as she will be able to provide differentiated literacy tasks, i.e. the right level of task for each learner.

Sally might also consider the content of the materials she is giving them to complete. The Adult Literacy Core Curriculum (2001) is an excellent tool for helping tutors to plan literacy sessions. It provides example activities and direction on how this might be delivered to groups of learners with varying abilities, but what it doesn't really tell us is how we may make the materials and activities as relevant as possible to our learners' interests and aspirations. Why is this important? Brown et al. (1998) tell us that learners are more likely to engage in learning if they are intrinsically interested in the material they are presented with. Providing materials that are relevant to the learner (as well as accessible) means that they are more likely to be intrinsically motivated and therefore more likely to engage in the learning process. For Sally, this means a number of things. She can decide to continue to provide literacy tasks that she sees as fit for purpose at the right level, or she can look at the learners' vocational programmes of study to see if she can make the literacy tasks she provides them with *vocationally relevant.* This means that Sally may provide the same types of literacy tasks at varying levels as indicated previously, but she might also design (or locate from pre-set materials) resources which are about motor vehicle maintenance and hairdressing. This may promote intrinsic interest in the learners and encourage them to complete the tasks.

The two actions outlined above will hopefully mean that the learners will participate in the completion of their tasks, remain engaged in learning and avoid such challenging behaviours as walking from the classroom or disrupting other learners by chatting. Sally is demonstrating some aspects of good practice by the use of the Adult Literacy Core Curriculum, which will provide her with guidance about providing differentiated activities in the same topic area, but she needs to do more research into the types of basic skills materials that have been developed to support the vocational curriculum if she hasn't the time to spend preparing her own.

The individual students

James

The task Sally gave James to complete was too easy for him. He completed it very quickly and then had nothing to do but chat to the other students. Sally interprets this as James being challenging towards her and, technically, disruption through talking is considered to be an aspect of challenging behaviour. However, if Sally takes a step back from this situation and identifies the causes of this behaviour, James' situation is relatively easy to deal with. If Sally applies just one of the group strategies as described above and provides James with a task that is at the right level for him, it will engage him in learning for the whole session, leaving him with no time to disrupt the other learners. Sally may also consider strategy two. Making the resources vocationally relevant will make the completion of the task more enjoyable for James as he has an intrinsic interest in the subject.

David

Based on Sally's reflections, David seems to be a willing student. He has 'given the sessions a go' but finds that he is not enjoying them and can't see the point. His challenge to Sally is in threatening not to attend any more sessions. This is based in the fact that he can't see the relevance of what he is being given to complete and he has become demotivated. The level of work that Sally provided to David seemed to be at the right level, so what Sally should do in order to help the situation is employ strategy two from above. If she does this she might find David more willing to participate, and like James, he might begin to see the relevance and point of the sessions.

Robert

At a cursory glance, we may say that Robert is demonstrating unacceptable and challenging behaviour. But Sally needs to reflect on the reasons why the student did not make any effort to participate in the session: there could be any number of reasons. Sally's frustration with Robert is understandable, but was challenging him directly in front of the other learners the right strategy to employ? Sally also seems to be making assumptions about the motor vehicle students. Why can we say this? Sally's referring to 'Jayne seeming nice' could infer that Sally is in danger of stereotyping the motor vehicle students. It is not uncommon for male students who are studying vocational programmes such as construction and motor vehicle studies to be labelled as students who are challenging in their behaviour, as rowdy and only interested in practical workshop tasks. Could Sally's views of the learner be clouded by her preconceptions? Finally, Sally's immediate reflection is that she will provide Robert with the same task next week. Is she likely to engage Robert in the next session if she does this, or is she potentially placing herself in a situation where there may be further conflict? Sally needs to review her strategy with the student before the next session. If she carries out the previous group strategies she will be able to provide him with an appropriate level and type of task and she may find him more willing to participate in the session. In addition to this, Sally might ask to meet with Robert before the next session to clear the air and to try to establish if there are any other issues she needs to be aware of. The student may be having problems at home, may have a learning difficulty Sally is unaware of or just might have been feeling ill that day. If Sally identifies any of these things it will make her more aware of any outside issues in Robert's life that might affect his behaviour in the classroom and this should enable her to adapt her strategies accordingly. She may also reconsider 'reporting' Robert in this instance, as this may just add to any feelings of anxiety or resentment he may be having. What is important is that Sally avoids getting into a conflict situation with Robert again, if at all possible. If none of these strategies work with Robert and he continues in non-participation, she may then have to consider seeking outside help in order to resolve the matter or seek some continuing professional development which may provide her with alternative strategies.

Jayne

Is Jayne presenting challenging behaviour? Not in the conventional sense perhaps, but the challenge for Sally is that she has had a student for a whole session who worked diligently but who clearly could not read what was in front of her. Why didn't Jayne say something to Sally? There could be many reasons: embarrassment, reluctance to admit in front of her male contemporaries that she couldn't read the task, or reluctance to expose her difficulties to a teacher she has only just met and with whom she has yet to form any kind of bond. Let's look at the information Sally has to work with to prepare her for her next session with Jayne. She thinks that Jayne might have a learning difficulty. Sally needs to find out what this is by contacting Jayne's personal tutor. Sally finds out that Jayne has Irlen Syndrome and usually uses coloured filters over her work when reading. Sally knows nothing about this syndrome so she looks it up on the internet. She finds out that Irlen Syndrome is a specific type of perceptual problem which affects the way the brain processes visual information. It is not caused by a problem with the eyes but the brain, which is unable to process the full spectrum of light. The use of coloured overlays enables the brain of learners with Irlen Syndrome to process and interpret the information they are reading. Why did Jayne not use her overlays in the classroom? Sally arranges to meet with Jayne before the next session to discuss this. It turns out Jayne had forgotten that she had a literacy class that day and had just been expecting to be working in the salon. She had been embarrassed and afraid to say that she had a problem in the previous session with being unable to read the exercises. She had her overlays today and although she was anxious about using them in front of the other learners, she would see how the session went. Sally may have other issues to deal with in the session if the other learners are overly interested in Jayne's coloured overlays.

Sally had time to reflect on the issues she came across in her classroom and time to develop a practical plan of action she could put in place for the following session. This is often the case for us as teachers and trainers in the Lifelong Learning sector. But sometimes we need to be able to deal with issues of challenging behaviour and conflict in the classroom as they arise (this is explored further in Chapter 6). For this reason it is useful to have a framework to work within in order for us to be better able to identify the precursors or antecedents to challenging behaviour and how we might then deal with them. Firstly we will look at the ABC model to promote behaviour change and then we will explore some strategies for managing conflict situations which can often arise as a result of challenging behaviour.

RESEARCH FOCUS RESEARCH FOCUS RESEARCH FOCUS RESEARCH FOCUS RESEARCH FOCUS

School discipline in the United Kingdom: promoting classroom behaviour which encourages effective teaching and learning

A research paper published by Sean Cameron in 1998 explored the use of the ABC model to promote positive behaviour after it was introduced into schools in the UK. It had very positive outcomes in changing negative to positive behaviour in the schools involved. The ABC model is a three-dimensional approach to the management and change of behaviour. Within the model, A is for *Antecedents,* B is for *Background (or context)* and C is for *Consequences*. Antecedents are the events or activities which happen before or leading up to the behaviour occurring. Antecedents are also sometimes called *triggers*. The Background is what is happening *around* the situation, the context of the behaviour and what can be done either to maintain it or change it. Consequences are what occur as a result of the behaviour. Consequences can be both positive and negative, such as praise to reinforce and reward acceptable behaviour and negative to reinforce unwanted behaviour. This model is now used increasingly in Lifelong Learning settings.

Managing behaviour in the classroom

Let's take the above model and apply it to a real situation that can commonly occur in the classroom. The following case study describes a trainee tutor's experience in teaching a group of students who have a range of LDDs. It highlights some of the challenges and pitfalls that teachers and trainers can make in dealing with a difficult situation in the classroom. The case study is followed by a discussion.

CASE STUDY 1
Foundation studies learners in FE

Rebecca is on an in-service part-time CertEd/PGCE in Teaching in the Lifelong Learning Sector and she has recently been given responsibility for a group of foundation studies students on a vocational programme. The students are based in an annexe away from the main college building which is quite isolated. One of the classrooms has a comfy low seating area for the students to relax on at break time. The rest of the room is set up with computers and working tables arranged in groups and a whiteboard. Rebecca has been told that the group contains some students who are challenging and difficult to manage. On entering the classroom for the first time, Rebecca finds that the learners have been let into the building by the caretaker. She finds that several of the students are sitting in the comfy seated area. They have their feet on the chairs and are conducting a conversation. The remaining students are sitting at the desks in preparation for the session to begin. Rebecca asks the students in the comfy chairs to come across to the working desks. She writes her aims and objectives on the whiteboard. As she is doing this a ball of paper hits the board beside her head. She turns around to find the group she asked to move still in the corner. She asks who threw the ball of paper; the group in the comfy chairs snigger, no name is forthcoming. Rebecca once again asks the students to come across to the working desks more forcefully this time. They reluctantly move across and sit at the desks in two separate groups of four. Rebecca starts her session. She delivers the session content as needed and then sets the students off on a task to complete. One group of learners (from the comfy seating area) do not attempt to complete the task and spend the rest of the session laughing and joking, and each time Rebecca turns to note things on the board she gets another ball of paper thrown in her general direction. There are also balls of paper being thrown at the other learners as they are trying to complete their work and one of the quieter students in the group, who has been hit with a ball of paper, gets upset and begins to cry. By the end of the session Rebecca has become extremely anxious and upset. She feels that the learners in the group that needed help have not been given it. She asks the disruptive student group (one of which is responsible for throwing the paper balls) to stay behind as she wants to talk to them. They remain, but as she tries to talk to them she is becoming more anxious and upset and they refuse to identify who threw the balls of paper and eventually refuse to answer her questions at all. In the end she lets them go, but she is extremely shaken by the experience.

Case study 1 discussion

What Rebecca has experienced, although upsetting, is behaviour that she is likely to come across if she continues to work with groups of learners including students with some of the more severe behavioural difficulties. What Rebecca needs is a plan of action for the next session to try to control the unwanted behaviours she experienced in the first session. She does some reading and comes across the ABC model for behaviour change. She draws herself a table in an effort to help her focus on the problem and search for solutions. The table overleaf shows what she concludes.

The table is not a catch-all, and it may not solve all of Rebecca's problems, but hopefully it will give her a basis to move forward with the learners and create an environment where there is less unwanted behaviour. Rebecca may find herself completing this activity each time she has taught the students. This could end in two ways: Rebecca will move all of the learners in the group in the direction she wants, or she will eventually isolate the main cause of the trouble (which in the above case may be one learner) and seek outside help in dealing with this.

Summary of my problems – What is the behaviour I am trying to change?	
The students sitting in the comfy corner.	
The students refusing to leave the comfy corner.	
Throwing paper balls at me or others when I am not looking.	
Sitting with friends and not working.	

ABC analysis	**My plan for the next session**
What are the antecedents to the behaviour? Getting into the annexe before me, they have control of that environment.	Make sure that the caretaker is told not to let the students into the annexe and to wait for me.
Having access to paper when they are not needing it to write on (paper in the corner near the comfy chairs).	Collect the paper and anything else lying around the comfy seating area and put it out of the way. Only have the resources needed for the session available and keep them on my desk till they are needed.
Sitting with friends (or their peer group) when they are at the desks, they won't give the culprit away and are probably egging him on.	Have a seating plan. Split them up so that they are not sitting together but are embedded in other groups. This might change the behaviour as the peer pressure will be different, and the paper-throwing culprit (if it occurs again) will be easy to pinpoint as the four students will be sitting at desks some distance apart. Also the behaviour of the peers might improve the behaviour of the culprit!
The laughter of their peer group.	Keep them apart as above.
If they saw I was getting upset it probably gave them confidence to continue (again peer group confidence). The same might be said for them upsetting the other students.	Keep my cool, stay in control and if things don't go according to plan, stay calm. Making them sit with the others might again help with this.
What about the background/context? How is that contributing to the problem behaviour? The annexe is away from the main college building. it doesn't feel like part of the college at all at times.	If things don't improve I could ask for them to be relocated in the main building where there will be a lot of staff about and classes going on all around them.
The learner is in a group of peers who will protect him. They are managing to sit with who they want and where they want.	Again, have a seating plan and direct them to where I want them to sit when they enter the classroom.
What can I find out about them from others who have taught the group?	If I know more about them it might help me to understand the reasons behind the behaviour.
What are the consequences of the behaviour? At the moment I have students not getting the attention they need.	I should be able to divide my attention more evenly and I might be given opportunities to reinforce good behaviour for all of the learners in the group (hopefully).
The problem group were kept back after session.	I hopefully won't need to keep them back for a telling off. This is a positive thing for all.
I lost control of the group, they were in control.	I hopefully will feel in control of the session throughout.

THEORY FOCUS THEORY FOCUS THEORY FOCUS THEORY FOCUS THEORY FOCUS

Managing conflict

There are strategies that can be used to manage situations of conflict through to resolution. Acceptable resolutions are normally best reached by a problem-solving approach (Crawford and Bodine, 2005), where the ultimate outcome is to turn conflict to resolution, with both parties content with the outcome. The problem-solving approach to conflict resolution involves a mediator who takes the lead in managing the conflict situation. Together they go through the following process:

1. Define the problem objectively.
2. Declare the need, why is this a problem?
3. Describe the feelings.
4. Discuss solutions, weigh the pros and cons of each solution.
5. Decide on a plan, use the solution that makes the most sense.
6. Determine the plan's effectiveness with a follow-up meeting.

Read the following excerpt from Samantha's teaching log. For part of her teaching practice she is team teaching with an experienced teacher in the student catering restaurant.

CASE STUDY 2

Managing student conflict

Today was very interesting. Two students, Ben and Holly, were having a stand-up row near the coffee bar in the college restaurant. Ben had been told off for not taking the menus round the tables as he had been instructed to do. Ben was furious with Holly as she had said to him she would help him to do this, but apparently she had been sent to work behind the coffee bar before she had had the chance. The tutor, Paul, intervened and took the students into a quieter part of the building to talk to them. I was asked along to help (well really to observe, I think) how he dealt with the situation. He asked the students what was wrong, they told him what had happened, he asked them to describe how they felt. Ben said he felt angry and let down, Holly said she felt bad about it, but she had been moved before she got a chance to talk to Ben. Paul said that he couldn't have them arguing in the restaurant, so what was the solution going to be? Holly said that she didn't want to argue with Ben but he had to accept she hadn't done it on purpose. Ben said she could have sent someone with a message for him so he could have completed the job himself, but he understood she hadn't done it deliberately. They both agreed that if it happened again in the future they would somehow get a message to the other and then the problem wouldn't arise. Both students were happy with this.

Case study 2 discussion

What Paul has done is take the students through the process of conflict resolution as described previously. He has taken the students from a position of conflict to a 'win-win' situation. Take a few minutes to reflect on this. Have you advertently or inadvertently gone thorough this process yourself with learners who have been in a conflict situation? If not, consider applying this process when you encounter situations of conflict with students.

Can challenging behaviour ever be positive?

Rebecca's experiences in a previous case study in this chapter were certainly not positive, but sometimes what can feel like challenging behaviour or a challenge to our authority as the tutor or trainer can be something as straightforward and innocent as a student testing out the extent of their own knowledge and understanding. Although at first glance this might feel like a challenge to the tutor or trainer's authority, it may, in reality, be the opposite. What is important to remember in these situations, especially with older learners, is that they have a wealth of life experience that they will bring to their learning and will have established principles and ideas of their own. If handled skilfully by the tutor, heated discussions (one might say a situation of conflict) are not always a bad thing. According to Wingert and Molitor, classroom conflict can lead to rich and productive learning if it is managed effectively. The key to success in this type of learning situation is the management of the situation by the tutor or trainer.

CLOSE FOCUS **CLOSE** FOCUS **CLOSE** FOCUS **CLOSE** FOCUS **CLOSE** FOCUS

Celeste is in a relatively mature group of learners. All are between 20 and 50 years old and are completing a foundation degree in early childhood studies as part of their ongoing continuing professional development. Consider the following scenario, which has three different endings.

Scenario

Celeste is delivering a presentation as part of her course work. At the end of the presentation the students are encouraged to ask questions of Celeste. One student challenges Celeste as to the accuracy of some of the detail in her presentation, and as Celeste looks a little flustered...

Ending 1

...the tutor steps in and tries to answer the question for her in order to avoid a potential situation of conflict arising. Celeste seems unhappy at the tutor's interference.

Ending 2

...and thinks about this for a while, another student in the group (a friend of Celeste) asks the questioner what she means. The questioner retorts that it's obvious, then Celeste joins in the discussion which deteriorates into an argument, the three learners talking loudly at the same time so no one can hear what is being said. The tutor asks them to stop and sends the class on a break to give the situation time to calm down. The three stomp out of the classroom.

Ending 3

...she turns to her friend for support. Celeste's friend is about to say something to the questioner when the tutor steps in and asks her to wait. The tutor, who has been observing Celeste, realises that all Celeste needs is a little time to reflect on what has been asked so that she can answer the question herself. Once Celeste has responded to the question, the tutor asks Celeste's friend for her contribution to the discussion. Following this, she throws the whole debate open to the class, managing effectively to provide everybody with a chance to contribute. By the end of the discussion Celeste has some interesting viewpoints to help her reflect on the content of her presentation. The original questioner has also reflected and taken on the viewpoints of Celeste and understands them more, though she still might not agree with them all. Celeste's friend was able to support her in a managed situation which enabled a sensible whole-class debate to begin. At the end of the session the classroom is buzzing and all of the learners leave in happy and motivated frames of mind.

Discussion

Which of the above endings to the scenario do you think provided the best outcome for learning and the learners and why?

Ending 3 gave the best outcomes in terms of providing a rich learning experience for all of the learners in the classroom. The teacher stepped in at the right time and provided appropriate direction by the use of good classroom management skills. This guided the three learners from a potential situation of conflict not only to a win-win situation, where negative feelings were nullified, but into a healthy debate that engaged all of the class in learning and which all of them were likely to reflect upon positively following the session. Ending 1 provided the second-best outcome. Although the learners were not provided with the opportunity to really question Celeste, at least a situation of conflict was avoided. However, this was a missed opportunity for the tutor or trainer who in this instance perhaps didn't feel skilled enough or brave enough to take the risk of seeing how the situation would develop. Inexperienced tutors and trainers often wish to avoid situations of conflict, but this does not always lead to the best learning outcomes, especially with groups of adult learners who can learn much from each other given the opportunity. Ending 2 provided the worst outcome for everyone, with situations of conflict not resolved between the three main players, the rest of the group being excluded from the discussion and the tutor probably feeling that the situation had got out of control. In addition to this, the unresolved situation might spill over into the remainder of the session after the break and future sessions potentially if the tutor does not handle the returning students carefully.

A summary of classroom management strategies

This section provides a list of strategies and tips that give guidance on managing situations of challenging behaviour.

- If trying to resolve situations of challenging behaviour, use a framework to help the analysis of what is happening, such as the ABC model.
- Seek outside help, for example a mentor or more experienced tutor, if needed.
- Agree behaviour management procedures with other staff. If all are applying the same strategies consistently it will help to promote behaviour change.
- Take control from the beginning, set the parameters of behaviour by setting the tone for the session at the start.
- Make the room work for you. Organise your teaching room to provide you with the best opportunities to manage the classroom as you want it to be and promote the types of behaviours you want to see.
- If the room isn't working for you, seek alternative accommodation.
- Look for signals from students that a problem is coming.
- Where possible, anticipate and remove the problem situation.
- Try to engage the whole group. Get commitments through contracts if necessary.
- Keep the learners busy by providing appropriately differentiated tasks.
- Constantly monitor learners' progress, provide regular feedback and encourage learner input.
- Make yourself available to talk with learners who seem to have issues.
- Make sound judgements: is it a positive or a negative challenge? Will it be detrimental to the learning experience or could it add to the learning experience? Remember, appropriate types of challenges can greatly enrich the learning experience for all involved if managed effectively by the tutor or trainer.

- Develop behaviour management skills and skills in managing conflict such as:
  - using direct instruction rather than questions. For example, 'Don't do that';
  - reducing physical distance and using eye contact;
  - not asking questions more than twice;
  - using a soft but firm voice;
  - giving enough time for the learner to respond to your request;
  - using start requests instead of stop ones. For example, 'Please can you start that task I asked you to do?' as opposed to 'Stop that! Haven't you got a task to do?';
  - making non-emotional descriptive requests;
  - consistently reinforcing desired behaviours with praise;
  - modelling appropriate behaviour at all times.

A SUMMARY OF **KEY POINTS**

In this chapter we have looked at the following key points:

> **we have explored what constitutes challenging behaviour and identified and discussed some of the underlying causes of this;**

> **we have looked at a range of strategies that can be employed to manage challenging behaviour and situations of conflict and thus promote a more inclusive learning environment;**

> **we have discussed some of the implications of challenging behaviour and situations of conflict on teaching and learning practices.**

REFERENCES AND FURTHER READING REFERENCES AND FURTHER READING

Books

Brown, S, Armstrong, A and Thompson, G (1998) *Motivating Students*. Birmingham: SEDA Publications.

Crawford, D and Bodine, R (2005) *Conflict Resolution in Education: a guide to implementing programs in schools, youth-serving organizations, and community and juvenile justice settings*. Honolulu, HI: University Press of the Pacific.

Journal articles

Cameron, R J (Sean) (1998) School discipline in the United Kingdom: promoting classroom behaviour which encourages effective teaching and learning. *Educational and Child Psychology*, 15(1): 40–55.

Wingert, D and Molitor, T (2009) Best Practices: Preventing and Managing Challenging Classroom Situations. *Currents in Teaching and Learning*, 1(2): 4–18.

Government publications

Department for Education and Skills (2001) *The Adult Literacy Core Curriculum*. London: DfES.

Websites

Irlen Syndome www.irlenuk.com/irlen-symptoms-overview.htm (accessed 9 February 2011).

5
Planning for an inclusive college

By the end of this chapter you should:

- have a developing, critical awareness of the implications of an inclusive approach to teaching and learning across institutions;
- have a critical understanding of current research-informed debates about inclusion and widening participation.

Professional Standards

This chapter relates to the following Professional Standards:

Professional Values:

AS 3 Equality, diversity and inclusion in relation to learners, the workforce and the community.

Professional Knowledge and Understanding:

AK 3.1 Issues of equality, diversity and inclusion.

FK 1.1 Sources of information, advice, guidance and support to which learners might be referred.

FK 1.2 Internal services which learners might access.

Professional Practice:

AP 3.1 Apply principles to evaluate and develop own practice in promoting equality and inclusive learning and engaging with diversity.

FP 1.1 Refer learners to information on potential current and future learning opportunities and appropriate specialist support services.

Introduction

In the course of the previous two chapters, our focus has been on classroom practice. But there is much more to working as a lecturer or tutor in a FE college or adult education centre than this. Tutors are increasingly expected to take on other roles and responsibilities as well. It is not uncommon for tutors to find themselves taking on responsibility for carrying out interviews and diagnostic assessments as part of the application and enrolment process. Many tutors are given responsibility for recruitment to and publicity for their course or programme of study. Tutors may have to liaise with other professional workers, such as learning support assistants, or with employers, or other people who might be sponsoring students in some way. And, as they are on the front line, it is often the tutor to whom students will turn first for advice or guidance – or complaint – about course fees, bursaries or transport. Within a FE college, being able to find the appropriate office to call in on, or the appropriate person to ask for help, is relatively commonplace: it is not too difficult for a tutor in FE to point a student towards someone who can provide advice about applying for additional funding or about accessing study skills support. But for those practitioners who work in community settings (in college outreach centres, for example, or adult education centres) or whose teaching practice involves working during anti-social hours (at weekends or during evenings), things can be more difficult. Being a teacher in these kinds of environments can feel very isolating (and we write this from experience): when you are one of only a very few people still working in an otherwise empty college, it is hard enough to find help if the photocopier jams, never mind find someone who can give well-informed advice to a student with a learning difficulty who would like to enrol on a course of study but has understandable reservations about their ability to cope.

In this chapter, therefore, we will think about all those ways in which tutors need to extend their professional roles beyond the walls of their workshops and classrooms. In this book, we argue that inclusive practice is about much more than 'just' planning and designing teaching activities and resources so that they meet the needs of a diverse learner group. It is also about creating a wider, cross-institutional environment that is inclusive, that feels open to everybody, and as such is an environment that needs to be established as soon as a student or potential student comes through the front door. Inclusive practice needs to be seen at work not only within teaching rooms, but also within a college (or any other kind of institutional setting – the title of this chapter is not meant to exclude adult education buildings, outreach centres, workplace settings and the like) as a whole.

If all this sounds like something that college managers, as distinct from tutors, should be busying themselves with, then that's because it is – to a certain degree. But just as the role of the teacher in the Lifelong Learning sector includes admissions, publicity, quality assurance and pastoral support, so it also involves knowing some things about learning support, about the financial help that might be available for students with LDDs, about assistive technology, and about learning and teaching strategies that can meet the needs of such diverse student groups. In the previous two chapters, our focus has been the classroom: now it is the wider institutional environment.

When considering the ways in which institutions respond more generally to an inclusive practice agenda, it is important to remember that audit processes, and Ofsted inspections in particular, provide one of the more powerful incentives for doing so. The Common Inspection Framework for Further Education and Skills (2009) foregrounds issues relating to, among other things:

- learners' social and economic well-being;
- the extent to which colleges and other institutions provide for social inclusion;
- the ways in which providers manage equality and diversity issues, with a particular stress on disability, gender and race;
- the extent to which providers work to increase participation from under-represented groups.

One of the more conspicuous ways by which colleges can negotiate these requirements is through the provision of courses that are presented in such a way that they are as accessible as they might reasonably be to as diverse a population as possible, ideally in a curriculum area that can be seen as aligned to possible areas for future employment or further training. Access courses provide a good example, and it is to one such course that we now turn.

CASE STUDY 1

Getting ready for the start of term

The following case study describes some of the actions carried out by a FE college tutor as she prepares for the start of the new academic year. The tutor, Theresa, is a tutor in health and social care, with particular responsibilities for the Access to Nursing course. As you read, think about the kinds of actions that might need to be taken to ensure inclusive practice, before considering the specific points that are raised by the case.

Preparing an information and enrolment evening for Access to Nursing

Nunthorpe College runs a number of access courses that allow students, upon successful completion, to transfer automatically to relevant courses that are offered at a nearby university. As such, these access programmes provide a way for 'non-traditional' students, as Theresa tends to refer to them in staffroom discussions or other more formal meetings with fellow tutors, to go into higher education. There are no formal entry criteria for the access course, and admissions decisions are made by the tutor – Theresa – on the basis of an interview, as well as through a consideration of any prior qualifications or relevant experience the applicant may have. Often she will also ask applicants to complete a short piece of written work, on a negotiated topic, that can act as a form of diagnostic assessment. Theresa has decided to hold an evening event (although the Access to Nursing course is run both during the day and in the evening) that will combine a standard 'open evening' with course advice and enrolment. She has booked a seminar room for the event, and has arranged the chairs and tables in rows facing a smart board, which she can use to display key information about the course. Near the door, she has set up a couple of tables on which she has put multiple copies of the college prospectus, a course information guide that relates specifically to the access programme, application forms, copies of the prospectus for the daycare nursery that is attached to the college, local bus timetables, and copies of a leaflet produced by the college titled Financial Support for Students.

Issues to consider

From the outset, it is important to note that Theresa has planned activities that are well thought through and appropriate to the requirements of the courses that she teaches. Most importantly, these activities also demonstrate that she has considered a range of issues relating to the progress and welfare of the students. Access courses are almost by definition the very embodiment of an inclusive approach, offering as they do creative routes into higher education for 'non-traditional' students, or students who are seen as being 'under-represented' in universities. The flexibility of the entry criteria for the Access to Nursing course that Theresa looks after require that she exercises both professional judgement and autonomy. The effect of this is to make the recruitment and admissions process an important element of the initial assessment process: this is not 'just' a college open evening. But if we were to look at the evening from a critical, inclusive practice perspective, what kinds of issues would emerge? Three themes come out of this case study, all of which may seem at first relatively prosaic, but which in fact hint at more profound themes.

1 Labelling students as 'non-traditional' (or, indeed, as anything else)

The ways in which students – or anybody – are described or 'labelled' can have profound consequences for how they are treated or viewed in a wider sense. That is to say, it is somehow as a result of the labelling process that particular characteristics or qualities are attached to people in ways that may not be justified. Such labels can be informal: for example, when a member of staff refers to a student as 'difficult', other tutors may then be predisposed to interpret aspects of that student's behaviour as 'difficult' or 'troublesome' when in fact the behaviours in question may indicate something quite different, such as an unrecognised or undiagnosed learning difficulty. Other labels can be more formal, such as when a student is given a statement of SEN. In cases such as this, tutors may 'see' the statement first, and the student second: their responses to and understanding of that student will in some way be filtered through the fact that she or he has received a statement.

So what is a 'non-traditional' student and, more importantly, what are the consequences of referring to a group of students as 'non-traditional'? There are two common answers to this. Firstly, if an applicant to a course or programme of study does not possess the entry qualifications that are usually required by the admissions criteria of the course in question, then the applicant is 'non-traditional' or 'non-standard'. Secondly, if the applicant is older than the students who make up the majority of the cohort for the course in question then the applicant is again 'non-traditional', an 'adult learner' or a 'mature student'. Put simply, they are different.

And it is in this attribution of difference that the problem can be found. In Chapter 2, we discussed the ways in which definitions of disability have changed over time, and considered the ways in which people describe – or label – people with disabilities have also changed. Instead of defining disability from a starting point of what people cannot do (a deficit model), more contemporary and inclusive definitions start from a point of view of what people can do, or could do if particular disabling barriers were removed. Arguably, describing an Access to Nursing group as 'non-traditional' or even 'non-standard' is also, in its own way, disabling. It reinforces images of students who lack study skills, who lack prior formal education and who have somehow failed during earlier stages of their educational careers. But if we start from a perspective of what students on such access courses can do, then a more positive and affirmative picture emerges: of people who have taken time away from formal learning to look after young children or sick relatives; of people who have overcome trauma in their personal lives and are now able for the first time to engage meaningfully with education and training; of people who through no fault or deficit of their own were unable to achieve before, but are now able to make the most of a second chance that is being offered to them. And how often have we heard the FE sector referred to as the 'second chance' sector?

What does all of this mean for our understanding of inclusive practice and the wider role of the institutional environments within which we work? Put simply, it means that we always have to treat and understand all of our students as individuals, with their own more or less complicated histories, biographies and identities. There are no students who are 'different' or 'normal' or 'traditional' or 'stereotyped': there are just students who are all individuals, and who need to be spoken to and responded to on their own terms.

2 Diagnostic assessment

Diagnostic, or initial, assessment can be understood as the process by which any appropriate assessment tool can be used to diagnose the entry behaviour or entry level of the applicant or student who is completing it. In many FE colleges, some forms of diagnostic assessment are applied across whole curricular areas: a commonly found example is the assessment of literacy and numeracy skills (using packages such as Basic and Key Skills Builder – BKSB). Sometimes, admissions tutors are able to exercise a degree of discretion, and ask applicants to complete a short essay or other piece of writing as part of the application process. Other activities or practices can also be seen as serving a diagnostic function. Application forms can provide admissions tutors with all sorts of useful information about the applicant, and not just because the applicant will have written down details about prior qualifications or prior work experience. The ways in which personal statements are written (the quality of handwriting, the grammar, the accuracy of the spelling) can also help tutors assess the literacy levels of the applicants. And it is important to be aware of factors such as these when considering entry to an Access programme where different kinds of academic writing may be required. Interviews, although they can be time-consuming, provide admissions tutors with the opportunity to talk with prospective students about their motivation for doing a course, their prior studies or experiences, and any specific needs that may need to be addressed. In sum, we can see diagnostic assessment as working in two ways: firstly, as part of a process of initial advice and guidance; and secondly, as part of a process of establishing whether a candidate meets the entry criteria for the course that she or he is interested in.

For students with disabilities, open evenings and interviews can provide an excellent opportunity to speak with prospective tutors, and it is important that tutors make the most of such opportunities whenever they are afforded to us. It is not uncommon for tutors to be 'surprised' when meeting new groups of students: sometimes we find ourselves teaching larger or smaller groups than expected, or teaching to a different syllabus or set of specifications. Sometimes we might find that the classroom allocations have all been rearranged, or that the classroom PC does not support the kinds of video files that we were intending to show to our students. And sometimes we might find that one or more of our students have a disability or difficulty that we either did not know about, or about which we are relatively ill informed.

We (Sharon and Jonathan) have been fortunate to work with very diverse groups of students during our years as teachers in both FE and HE, and we have invariably found that it is through speaking to students themselves that we have been best able to plan for inclusive teaching and learning. And many of our CertEd/PGCE students have had similar experiences. On many occasions, such conversations take place during termtime, after the course has started. This is of course a good thing, but if we consider the time that it can take to arrange for learning support workers or assistive technologies to be installed, then the importance of being able to have such conversations before the course starts would seem to be self-evident.

For some students, however, more complex arrangements may be needed, such as the provision of multiple additional members of staff, or of transport to and from college. Some students may require significant changes to the 'standard' assessment routine for their programme of study (and we shall return to this subject in Chapter 7). Adjustments and provisions such as these – and others – can be complex to arrange, taking both time and expertise that tutors do not necessarily possess. Nor are they expected to: one of the central messages of this book is that tutors need to be aware of and sensitive to an inclusive approach, but they cannot be expected to know as much about dyslexia as would a tutor with a specialist qualification, or about making adjustments for a student with impaired mobility as would an experienced learning support worker. These processes of negotiation, of finding out what resources and facilities are available, can all take time and can all usefully be started at the interview/application stage.

But it is important to note that for some potential students, an open/application evening such as the one that Theresa has organised may not provide the most appropriate opportunity for being able to demonstrate that the course in question is the right one for them, and that they have the potential to succeed. Students with mental health difficulties, for example, may find such interview situations to be highly stressful, and may well not 'perform' at their best as a result. In addition, they may have to take medication, with possible side-effects including losses in concentration or attention, which could also affect interview or diagnostic test performance. Students with impaired mobility or who are partially sighted may find a computer-based assessment difficult to complete without assistive technology.

Put simply, the running of open evenings or interview and recruitment sessions needs to be planned as carefully as you would plan any other learning and teaching session, so that it is, as far as practicable, inclusive to anyone who might wish to attend, and so that if someone turns up who does require assistance or support in any way, you are able either to provide it yourself, or point the student towards someone else who can. And very often, it will be the college disability support office, or learning support department, or whatever it is called within your institution, that can help.

3 Practical matters: times, places and spaces

Among people who teach, or do research into the lives of, adult learners, broad conversations about those factors that constitute barriers to participation often turn to specific discussions about the buildings or campuses that colleges or adult education centres occupy. That is to say, something to do with the actual buildings – the doors, the gates, the room – acts as a barrier to adults who may be wishing to return to learn. There are several issues to consider here. Some of these are purely practical or logistical: it may be the case that the public transport links to the college are difficult to negotiate, or that the college is too far away from the primary school attended by the children of the prospective student. But others are more cultural, even psychological. For some adult returners, particularly those for whom compulsory schooling was a negative experience, what the rest of us might see as the simple act of stepping through the front door constitutes a significant act: the look and feel of a FE college can be off-putting (even if it's one that has only recently been built). According to our broad model of inclusive practice, therefore, we can go on to consider these issues as being of relevance to the participation of not only adult returners, but also SEN students, students with seen or unseen disabilities, or students from disadvantaged social or economic backgrounds. What buildings are actually like, what sort of public transport exists, or how long it takes to get there, are factors which are as potentially disabling as other factors such as lift and ramp access, accessible facilities (catering, libraries, computer rooms) and designated parking bays for people with disabilities.

What are the practical and logistical aspects of Theresa's recruitment/admissions evening? There are, in fact, a few things to think about here: the way in which the session has been timed, the provision of resources and the arrangement of the room.

When running CertEd/PGCE classes in the evening, we (Sharon and Jonathan) have often allowed the group to finish a bit early so that people can catch an earlier bus home (and many other tutors do the same thing). If students rely on public transport, and finishing a class ten minutes early means that they can avoid a 30-minute wait for the next service, then finishing early seems to us to be an appropriate step to take. And at the same time, other students will want to hang around and talk on a one-to-one basis, or ask specific questions about an upcoming assignment. This is not to say that timetables and schedules are not important, because they are. But as teachers and trainers, we need to be realistic and to anticipate that our students will want to talk to us outside class contact time, and so we need to take reasonable steps to make ourselves available. If we are planning our teaching with such flexibility, it seems perfectly appropriate to consider other aspects of our professional behaviour in the same way, including recruitment and admissions events.

Theresa's event planning has much to commend it. 'Typical' access students tend to attend classes in the evening, and so the provision of an evening recruitment event is a logical step. The mixture of formal presentation with opportunities for more informal one-to-one conversations, the provision of prospectuses, course information guides and information about possible financial support all demonstrate quite clearly the thought and attention that she has put into her planning. At the same time, it could be argued that Theresa has not gone as far as she might in anticipating the needs of her potential students. All of the literature is in English (although they do all state, in multiple languages, that other versions are available); she has not planned a corresponding daytime recruitment session; there are no paper copies of her slides for people who miss the start of her presentation; and the way in which she has set out the room would make things awkward for someone with restricted mobility. But would it be *reasonable* to expect Theresa to have made these provisions?

It would have been straightforward for Theresa to provide paper copies of her presentation, in just the same way that it is reasonable for tutors to provide copies of teaching resources in advance of a taught session for the benefit of those students who need early access to such materials. Students with dyslexia, for example, may find it time-consuming to read Powerpoint slides, and being able to look at them in advance of the class would allow them time, in a relaxed environment, to study them. But in all other respects, she has provided as diverse a range of helpful materials as might reasonably be expected. And at the end of the evening, if some of the prospective students do require additional help or resources prior to making a decision as to whether to join the Access course, Theresa can – and is – willing to provide this on a negotiated basis.

Case study 1: Some concluding thoughts and reflections

This case study has been quite extensive in comparison to the others in this book. We have chosen to do this quite deliberately, in order to demonstrate the extent to which even something as straightforward as holding an open evening for potential students can raise all kinds of potentially problematic issues which tutors need to be aware of. It is unrealistic to expect tutors to anticipate everything, however: we cannot know who is going to attend a drop-in session, or predict the many kinds of behaviours or needs that they might exhibit. But through trying to create environments that are welcoming and providing lots of help relating to the kinds of issues that often create barriers to participation (in Theresa's case, ranging from where to obtain financial support, to finding childcare, to details about public transport), tutors can help make the very first moments of a student's journey supportive, positive and inclusive.

During the last ten years, FE colleges have been positioned by subsequent government initiatives as being at the forefront of promoting social inclusion, and one of the ways in which they are to achieve this is in reaching out to people who would not 'normally' go to college. As practitioners, we might argue that there are all kinds of benefits that returners might enjoy: social integration; the opportunity to meet new people and to enter new social networks; the chance to gain a formal qualification, perhaps for the first time; and to develop one's self-esteem. For governments, however, the focus of inclusion would seem to be to reintegrate people into mainstream education and give them the skills that they need to enter or re-enter employment. This is a definition of inclusion that requires a critical exploration, and so it is to this that we now turn.

RESEARCH FOCUS RESEARCH FOCUS RESEARCH FOCUS RESEARCH FOCUS RESEARCH FOCUS

Critical perspectives on social inclusion and the Lifelong Learning sector

To even the most casual observer of the politics of the post-16 education and training sector, the last 15 years (or so) can clearly be seen as a period during which the role or purpose of FE colleges in particular has been increasingly and successively defined as being to prepare people for the world of work at a time when that world has been changing rapidly. Instead of a college course or apprenticeship being a gateway to a 'job for life', colleges now have to deliver 'employability skills', 'key' or 'transferable' skills. At the same time, debates about the 'wider benefits of learning', while continuing to be heard among practitioners and academics, have (it could be argued) been increasingly ignored by policy makers.

In an article titled *Constructing Social Inclusion Through Further Education: the dangers of instrumentalism*, Joanna Williams of the University of Kent has argued that social inclusion has, over the last decade or so, been positioned by policy makers in terms of employability and as contributing to economic growth. She describes this approach as 'an instrumental model which focuses upon participation in the labour market as vital for social inclusion' (Williams, 2008, page 151), and goes on to argue that 'labour market participation is considered to bring about social inclusion through its role in sustaining financial independence and promoting the prosperity of individuals and families' (ibid., page 153). If governments tell us that social inclusion is linked to employability and that people need to improve their employability skills in order to keep up with a rapidly changing world economy, it therefore follows, Williams argues, that the position of governments is that it is down to individuals to get the skills they need. In a powerful conclusion, she states:

> This construction of social inclusion in terms of employability skills has a number of consequences: it shifts the focus away from structural economic concerns with industrial development and places it upon individuals. Individuals come to be held responsible for their own employability and consequently their own social inclusion. [...] In this way, low skills come to replace low income (or poverty) as the key marker of social exclusion.
>
> (Williams, 2008, page 158)

How do you respond to this argument? Is it the case that inclusion is 'only' about employability skills and helping people to get back to work? Or should 'inclusion' be about more than this? When starting your CertEd or PGCE course, did you think that being a teacher in the Lifelong Learning sector was 'just' about preparing your students for the world of work, or are there wider benefits to learning?

Terms such as inclusive practice or widening participation are commonplace within education and training environments, even if policy makers, college principals and academics do not always agree on what they actually mean. But just because there is one definition of inclusive practice, which Williams refers to as *instrumental*, that is championed by govern-ment ministers (and, in turn, by funding agencies), it need not be the only definition that we – as teachers and trainers – subscribe to or draw on in order to inform and reflect on our professional practice. The broader, more generous, definition of inclusive practice with which we started this book provides a sound and well-balanced alternative that is – we would argue – rooted within definitions of education, teaching and learning that are about more than just skills for the workplace. In fact, many colleges manage quite successfully to reconcile the need to deliver the kinds of courses that government funding agencies and employers expect (and we shall return to the curriculum in Chapter 7) with a broader, more inclusive approach to the local communities that they serve. Indeed, such an approach is frequently publicised in prospectuses, charters and mission statements.

PRACTICAL TASK PRACTICAL TASK **PRACTICAL TASK** PRACTICAL TASK **PRACTICAL TASK**

Communicating an inclusive message

FE colleges or workplace training providers often use mission statements to reflect the inclusive practice agenda. This is hardly surprising, as it is the source of considerable political – and financial – debate. Here are just two examples of mission statements from FE colleges:

> *The College's values are the development of a fully integrated learning community based around the programmes they are on in which students are treated according to their need, with parity of esteem irrespective of their background, race, gender, age, ambition, previous education and subject or level of study.*

> *To be the leading provider of high-quality education and training in the city and the surrounding area. This will be achieved by working in partnership with individuals and organisations to raise expecta-tions, fulfil potential and ensure a confident, economically successful and socially inclusive community.*

What messages do statements such as these convey? Are they messages that you, as a teacher or trainer in the Lifelong Learning sector, also subscribe to? Does the college or training centre where you work, or where you are on teaching placement, use a similar mission statement? Does your institution live up to the values that it espouses?

Despite the political and, especially, the financial pressures that many (if not all) FE colleges and adult education providers have to respond to, a significant number of providers within the post-16 sector continue to provide opportunities for education and training that serve the employability agenda and a more generously defined inclusion agenda as well. FE colleges, through the use of off-campus satellite venues, offer some of this provision. LEAs continue to offer education and training opportunities for young people as well as older adult retur-ners. However, at the time of writing this book, the financial pressures that post-16 educators are required to work around look set to increase considerably. When we also remember the cuts that have been made to 'adult responsive provision' within FE colleges over the last year or so, it might appear to be the case that social inclusion does indeed look to be increasingly focused solely on the 14–19 agenda (which we shall discuss in Chapter 7).

RESEARCH FOCUS RESEARCH FOCUS RESEARCH FOCUS RESEARCH FOCUS RESEARCH FOCUS

Critical perspectives on institutional barriers

There is a lot of published work (in both QTLS textbooks and in academic journals) focusing on the institutional barriers that can impede access to FE. 'Barriers to learning' is a common theme in teacher-training courses for the Lifelong Learning sector. But how much of a barrier do factors such as timing or transport *actually* create? In an article titled *Do barriers get in the way? A review of the determinants of post-16 participation*, Stephen Gorard and Emma Smith argued that the impact of these barriers could be both misunderstood and misrepresented. The article begins by synthesising a number of other pieces of research relating to participation, for example:

Institutional barriers to participation in post-compulsory education come from the procedures of the providing organisations themselves, in terms of advertisement, entry procedures, timing and scale of provision, and general lack of flexibility. Colleges of FE, for example, have traditionally assumed a 17-year-old norm and are having to adapt to more flexible opportunities for learning, because people often have interrupted patterns of participation and diverse progression routes.

(Gorard and Smith, 2007, page 146)

But they then go on to argue that:

The case presented for barriers does not provide evidence that overcoming barriers makes any difference in practical terms. For example, there is no evidence that Information and Communications Technology (ICT) attracts any new students who would not otherwise have enrolled, or that it makes their retention and success more likely.

(ibid., page 147)

Put simply, Gorard and Smith argue that simply offering bursaries and fee reductions, for example, does not in fact significantly increase participation in FE by people from economically disadvantaged backgrounds. Such initiatives fail to address more profound social inequalities, which are translated into educational inequalities in both compulsory and post-compulsory education or training.

Conclusion

Notwithstanding the valid points raised by Gorard and Smith in their research, it seems right to expect providers of education and training to establish and then sustain patterns of delivery that are flexible and responsive to the diverse needs of students. These must, of course, in some ways be responsive not only to the students themselves, but also to the needs of local communities, local employers and local social or economic pressures. But it would be a pity if the search for 'employability' (whatever that might be) were to be allowed to push a broader social inclusion agenda, based on a more emancipatory definition of inclusive practice, to one side. There has to be a push for skills, even though the link between an up-skilled workforce and national economic performance is far from proven. But there also has to be time for nurturing those students for whom social or cultural inclusion is about more than employability: rather, it is about taking part, about making use of the college as a local community or resource, about making friends when attending class and expanding one's horizons.

A SUMMARY OF **KEY POINTS**

In this chapter we have looked at the following key points:

> **approaches to inclusive practice that extend beyond the classroom;**

> **the ways in which students are labelled as 'different';**

> **inclusive approaches to diagnostic assessment;**

> **critical perspectives on inclusion, and on barriers to learning.**

Many of the issues raised in this chapter could be usefully expanded on, and we cannot hope to give more than a flavour of the complex debates that surround these issues. But what we hope this chapter does achieve is to raise awareness of, and sensitivity to, the many needs that students may have, and the complex histories that they bring with them.

REFERENCES AND FURTHER READING REFERENCES AND FURTHER READING

Gorard, S and Smith, E (2007) Do barriers get in the way? A review of the determinants of post-16 participation. *Research in Post-Compulsory Education*, 12(2): 141–58.

Williams, J (2008) Constructing social inclusion through further education: the dangers of instrumentalism. *Journal of Further and Higher Education*, 32(2): 151–60.

6
Inclusive learning and teaching practices

By the end of this chapter you should:

- have a developing understanding of how being a reflective practitioner can assist in the ongoing improvement of teaching and learning practices;
- have an increasing awareness of how adapting teaching and learning practices within the classroom can have a positive impact upon promoting inclusion;
- begin to appreciate how collaborative working can have a positive impact upon classroom practices.

Professional Standards

This chapter relates to the following Professional Standards:

Professional Values:

AS 1 All learners, their progress and development, their learning goals and aspirations and the experience they bring to their learning.

AS 3 Equality, diversity and inclusion in relation to learners, the workforce and the community.

AS 4 Reflection and evaluation of their own practice and their continuing professional development as teachers.

Professional Knowledge and Understanding:

AK 3.1 Issues of equality, diversity and inclusion.

DK 1.1 How to plan appropriate, effective, coherent and inclusive learning programmes that promote equality and engage with diversity.

AP 4.3 Share good practice with others and engage in continuing professional development through reflection, evaluation and the appropriate use of research.

AK 5.1 Ways to communicate and collaborate with colleagues and/or others to enhance learners' experience.

Professional Practice:

AP 3.1 Apply principles to evaluate and develop own practice in promoting equality and inclusive learning and engaging with diversity.

AP 5.1 Communicate and collaborate with colleagues and/or others, within and outside the organisation, to enhance learners' experience.

Introduction

This chapter considers the role of the tutor inside and outside of the classroom in supporting inclusive learning practices. While acknowledging at all times the need to defer to specialist staff, there is nonetheless a lot that tutors in the Lifelong Learning sector can do to be proactive, rather than reactive, in anticipating the diverse needs of students with seen or unseen disabilities, or with particular learning or support needs. This chapter provides both practical advice and a sound rationale for such inclusive approaches and these are considered and evaluated within conventional models of reflective practice. As students on Cert Ed/PGCE/DTLLS courses in Lifelong Learning settings, we spend time writing critically reflective evaluations of sessions we have delivered. We develop reflective journals which look in depth at a range of classroom issues and/or critical incidents that have occurred in our teaching and we are encouraged to do this so that we may identify not only where things have gone well in our teaching but also where we can improve our future teaching practices. Although this chapter is about being inclusive in our teaching practices, it also explores how the use of models of reflective practice can assist us in developing as practitioners.

RESEARCH FOCUS RESEARCH FOCUS **RESEARCH FOCUS** RESEARCH FOCUS **RESEARCH FOCUS**

What is reflective practice and why is it important?

John Dewey (1933) developed his notion of reflective teaching and this theory is still integral to reflective practice for teachers today. Dewey contrasted routine action, which he described as non-reflective, unresponsive action guided by tradition, habit and authority, with reflective action, which he described as a willingness to engage in constant self-appraisal and development, flexibility, rigorous analysis and social awareness. Dewey believed that good teachers use reflective action in order to improve their ongoing teaching practices. Donald Schön (1983) developed Dewey's notion of the reflective teacher further as he was not only concerned with reflection on practice 'after the event', which he called *reflection-on-action*, but also with how teachers used reflection while engaged in practice, the 'thinking on your feet' changes teachers make in their teaching activities in order to meet the needs of the learners at that time. He called this *reflection-in-action.*

To help us to relate this theory to practice, consider the following scenario where we find an experienced tutor, Stuart, adapting his practice to meet the needs of the learning group.

CASE STUDY 1

Adapting practice to promote inclusion

Stuart is delivering a session to a group of adult learners who are on an NVQ level 2 counselling programme. He doesn't know the group at all as he is covering the session for a colleague who is ill. He starts them off on an individual learning task following the teaching input, but as he walks around the classroom he notices that one or two learners seem to be struggling to complete it so he decides that the only way to include them all in the task is to turn it into a group discussion task. He abandons his plan for this part of the session and moves them into small groups of four. All of the students but one seem to be completing the learning task much more effectively. The learner who is struggling asks Stuart if he can continue and complete the individual task as it was originally set. He then tells Stuart that he is hearing-impaired and generally struggles to keep up in group discussions and that the regular tutor always plans for this by providing tasks that are appropriate. Stuart agrees that this is fine and he manages the classroom environment so that the hearing impaired learner can complete the task in a way which suits him as well as the other learners. Stuart then gives the learners an individual pre-set case study question as a formative assessment task. One student feeds back that she would find the completion of the task much more relevant if she could base her responses on a real-life case at her work. After exploring any ethical considerations with the learner, Stuart agrees she can do this. One or two others ask if they can do the same, which Stuart agrees to, while the remainder seem happy to continue using the pre-set study. Stuart lets them continue for a while, when he notices one learner who appears to be struggling. He sits with the learner and asks if he can help. The learner tells Stuart that he has dyslexia and struggles to read, understand and respond to things quickly, and if they can talk the question through together it will help him to understand what is required and he will be better able to answer the question. Stuart talks the case study through with the learner and checks on an ongoing basis that he is able to complete the task by providing prompts and direction to the learner as necessary.

Following the session Stuart makes some notes on his lesson plan. He makes a note of what he changed and why, reflecting that next time he might just have a pre-set case study as backup, and initially encourage the learners to use their own life experiences as this seemed to be very effective in promoting learning for the learners in the group that did this. He also ponders the initial individual task he gave them, which actually worked much better as a group learning activity for the majority of learners. He then considers the two learners in the group who had a learning difficulty and/or disability and is pleased that he managed to adapt his practices to make sure that they were as fully included in the learning process as possible, given the situation he was presented with.

Case study 1 discussion

At first glance it may seem that what Stuart did was relatively easy. He adapted his practices to meet the needs of his learners while in the classroom and then reflected on this after the session had finished. Does this make Stuart a reflective practitioner? If we look at Stuart's experiences and consider the reflective practice theory discussed earlier, we can conclude that Stuart has embraced both principles of Dewey's reflective action and Schön's reflection in and on action. For example, when Stuart realised that the individual task was not working as planned, he adapted this almost immediately to meet the needs of the learners at that time. By adapting it into a group activity, he applied *reflection-in-action.* He did this again when the hearing-impaired learner asked if he could continue the task as it was originally set. He adapted his practices again, and he managed the learning environment so that all of the learners could complete the task effectively, thus demonstrating inclusive practice. He did this again with the formative assessment task. He thought through the implications for the students who wanted to use their real-life experiences as a case study before making the decision that (for that small group of learners) learning would become more meaningful if he did so. He then demonstrated more *reflection-in-action* by once again adapting his class-room practices in order to provide the best chance for the learner with dyslexia to be included. Stuart did this by providing the learner with one-to-one help and the support he needed to complete the case study task. Following the session he engaged in *reflection-on-action.* He thought about what had happened in his classroom and as a result of this decided how this might affect his future teaching practices both generally and more specifically, if he had to take this group of learners again. He also demonstrated Dewey's notion of reflective action as he:

- has demonstrated a willingness to engage in self-appraisal and development;
- has demonstrated flexibility in his practices;
- has engaged in analysis of his practices and demonstrated awareness of what was happening in the classroom;
- has observed what was happening in the classroom and
- was constantly aware of both the groups and the individuals in the groups changing needs.

In summary, if Stuart had not practised reflection-in-action his session would not have turned out as successfully as it did, and because he is willing to engage in reflection on his practices and respond to areas of concern on an ongoing basis, he is more likely to be able to meet the needs of his learners in the future and be inclusive in his teaching practices.

As trainee tutors and trainers, we can often benefit greatly from working with experienced colleagues. One of the most effective ways of doing this is observing them in practice.

PRACTICAL TASK PRACTICAL TASK PRACTICAL TASK PRACTICAL TASK PRACTICAL TASK

Observing an experienced practitioner

As part of your continuing professional development, make arrangements to observe an experienced tutor. Make a note of any adaptations the tutor makes that you consider to be reflection-in-action. After the session, talk to the tutor about the changes they made and why.

Dealing with a range of different learning needs

As teachers and trainers in the Lifelong Learning sector, we will always have students accessing our programmes of learning who have differing needs, different abilities, expectations and aspirations. This means that if we want our practices to be as inclusive as possible we need to be aware of who our learners are and also what is happening in the classroom at all times. We also need to be able and willing to adapt our classroom practices in order to promote inclusion in learning. Before we look at some of the more focused or specific areas we can address to promote inclusive practice, for example the use of a TA in the classroom or the development of the more specialist skills, such as use of multi-sensory approaches to teaching and learning (Lee, 2002), there are some broader aspects of good classroom practice we can utilise.

THEORY FOCUS THEORY FOCUS **THEORY** FOCUS **THEORY** FOCUS **THEORY** FOCUS

Tomlinson (1997) suggests a number of strategies we can adopt as teachers and trainers throughout the delivery of our sessions that will support inclusion in the learning experience for all. Some of these strategies are summarised as follows:

- The teacher should effectively co-ordinate the use of time, space and activities.
- There should be flexible grouping which ensures fluidity of working arrangements that are consistent as far as possible.
- There should be a range of strategies such as whole-class learning, paired learning, small group learning, teacher-selected learning groups and random learning groups.
- Flexible use of time is needed to respond to the learners' needs at any given time.
- A wide variety of classroom management strategies are needed, such as independent study, interest groups, learning buddies and tiered assignments, in order to help to target instruction to the students' needs.
- There should be clear criteria for success developed at both group and individual level to provide guidance to the students as to what would be a successful learning outcome. This should be revisited with groups and individual learners frequently during the session.

- Formative and summative assessment activities should be varied to enable the learners to demonstrate their own thoughts and learning growth. These should be adapted as necessary within acceptable guidelines, particularly with summative assessment tasks.

What Tomlinson is telling us is that in order to be inclusive in our practices, not only do we need to be able to respond and react to what is happening in the classroom and adapt what we are doing, but we also need to use *reflection-in-action* to be proactive in our teaching practices. We need to be flexible and react to the learners' growth and development and we need to put the learners at the centre of this process in order for this to happen effectively. Complete the following reflective task. The purpose of this task is to encourage you to evaluate if and how you adapt your classroom practices to respond to the ongoing changing needs of your learners. It will help you to identify and evaluate where and if you are using *reflection-in-action.*

REFLECTIVE TASK

Think about a teaching session you have delivered recently. Did you stick rigidly to your lesson plan or did you adapt some of your activities as the lesson progressed? If you did not adapt anything, why was this? Was it because the session went absolutely according to plan and you were happy with the delivery? Maybe you are not confident and experienced enough as trainee tutors and trainers to adapt your planned activities, even if things are not going as you planned? Be honest when you reflect on these questions. Perhaps you could use them as a basis for an entry in your reflective journal.

Tomlinson provides us with some useful general tips about how we might make our lesson content more accessible by virtue of using a diverse range of teaching and learning strategies. What Tomlinson does not address is dealing with issues around inclusion for learners who have more specialist needs and the strategies that we as teachers and trainers in the Lifelong Learning sector can employ when learners with more complex difficulties join our programmes of learning. Consider the following case study. It is about Robert, a trainee teacher, and how he has to make plans to meet the needs of a learner with a visual impairment.

CASE STUDY 2

Robert and Sophie

Robert, a trainee teacher, has been approached by the college's co-ordinator for students with LLDs. The co-ordinator informs Robert that a student, Sophie, who is visually impaired, has been accepted on the course he has become programme leader for and that in a meeting held with Sophie to establish her needs the following information was agreed. Sophie requires handouts to be enlarged by 20%, she needs to be at the front of the teaching room and she has requested that a seat be kept near the front of the room for her. Sophie has also requested that, for as much time as possible, the tutor faces the front when delivering the content of the sessions to enable her to engage more fully with the teacher's delivery of the teaching content. It was also agreed that Sophie will be accompanied by a TA during teaching. This TA will take classroom notes and assist Sophie in the learning process in order to take care of her pastoral needs.

Robert is keen to support the student but he is unsure about the practicalities of achieving this aim. Robert decides to meet with Sophie to discuss ways of improving the educational experience. Robert also plans to meet with his practice mentor, an experienced tutor, for assistance and guidance at regular intervals during his delivery of the programme. This is in order to discuss practical advice in ensuring that Sophie is fully included in the learning process. Robert is aware that meeting Sophie's needs will at times mean extra preparation work for him, but he is keen to support Sophie's progress as much as possible.

Case study 2 discussion

Robert has been proactive in his planning in order to try to meet Sophie's needs so that she can be fully included in the learning process. Robert was approached by the co-ordinator for specific learning difficulties and provided with the information he required, but what Robert has done is taken this a step further. He has met with Sophie, which should make her feel less anxious when she begins her course, as Robert will have discovered if she has any additional requirements and he will also have made the very important initial connection with the learner that might have been difficult if he had waited for the first busy classroom session. He is also including his learning mentor in his deliberations and reflections, using his more experienced peer to help him to evaluate his practice and to discover ways in which he might help Sophie further. He acknowledges that having Sophie in his classroom will mean additional work for him, but he is willing to take this on in order to provide Sophie with the best learning experience possible. Do you think that Robert has engaged in reflective practice in his actions for Sophie? Consider the following seven principles of the reflective teacher and then re-evaluate Robert's activities with Sophie in light of these.

THEORY FOCUS **THEORY** FOCUS **THEORY** FOCUS **THEORY** FOCUS **THEORY** FOCUS

Dewey's reflective teacher

Dewey (1933) developed seven key characteristics of what reflective teaching is and what a reflective teacher should be and do. They are as follows:

1 Reflective teaching implies an active concern with aims and consequences as well as technical efficiency.

2 Reflective teaching is applied in a cyclical process in which teachers monitor, evaluate and revise their own practice continuously.

3 Reflective teaching requires competence in methods of evidence-based classroom enquiry to support the progressive development of higher standards of teaching.

4 Reflective teaching requires attitudes of open-mindedness, responsibility and wholeheartedness.

5 Reflective teaching is based on teacher judgement, informed by evidence-based enquiry and insights from other research.

6 Reflective teaching, professional learning and personal fulfilment are enhanced through collaboration and dialogue with colleagues.

7 Reflective teaching enables teachers to creatively mediate externally developed frameworks for teaching and learning.

We could say that Robert is being proactive and reflective in his endeavours to meet Sophie's needs, although he has not been in a classroom situation (and so has not had the opportunity to reflect upon his classroom practices with her). He is certainly demonstrating an active concern about the aims and consequences should he not prepare his session carefully to include Sophie. He is demonstrating open-mindedness, responsibility and wholeheartedness. He is collaborating with colleagues and he has been thinking about how he can adapt his practices creatively to include Sophie in the learning process as well as the other learners in the group. So how are Robert and Sophie progressing now that she has started her programme of learning?

CASE STUDY 3

Robert and Sophie six weeks on

Robert and Sophie are six weeks into the programme and all appears to be going well with his delivery. Robert initially struggled with some aspects of his classroom practice, such as forgetting to face the front as often as he could. He is also pleased that he seems to be coping well with the college's new initiative of reducing paper photocopying by use of the VLE. Now in his teaching he projects presentations, tasks and instructions for activities to be completed onto the white screen rather than providing paper copies to the learners. Sophie seems to be coping well with this. She hasn't said that it is a problem for her, and Robert assumes that everything she needs on paper is being provided by the TA prior to sessions. She is also joining in all classroom tasks with the TA's help. When Robert provides them with their first summative assessment task (which he projects onto the screen) and asks the learners to write it down, Sophie asks to be excused from the classroom. Robert can see that she is upset but is not sure why. He decides that he needs a one-to-one tutorial with Sophie to find out what is bothering her. When Robert meets with Sophie after the session she is clearly upset. She asks if she can speak to him without the TA being present, which surprises Robert but he agrees. Sophie tells him that she is very unhappy, that the TA does not provide her with the handouts she needs in the enlarged format but writes things down from the board which she then can't read. Sophie also feels that the TA is unclear about what is required of the tasks that are set in the classroom, so directs Sophie in a way that she feels is incorrect, but Sophie feels that she has no choice but to follow the directive of the TA. She tells Robert that if she had a laptop computer she could access the VLE and with appropriate help could enlarge the materials herself either before the session (if they were made available) or during the session if not. Robert tells Sophie that he is sorry that he didn't realise that Sophie was having problems and that he will address the concerns she has raised for the next session.

Case study 3 discussion

What has happened here is fairly typical of some of the issues that can arise when effective communication isn't happening between the key players in a learning situation. Robert has made assumptions about the TA's activities with Sophie, the TA may be feeling unsupported and unclear about what to do to support Sophie, and Sophie is left in the middle, unhappy and unclear about how she should take this situation forward. What lessons should Robert learn from this on reflection and how can he take the situation forward? The importance of effective communication between those responsible for providing Sophie with an inclusive learning experience cannot be under-estimated. More often than not, poor communication and a lack of joint planning will lead to situations as described above. So what should Robert do?

- First and foremost, he should plan to meet with the TA to discuss what is going wrong and to get her viewpoint.
- He should arrange to spend some joint planning time with the TA. This should happen before every session if possible. According to *Supporting the Teaching Assistant: a good practice guide* (DfES, 2000), joint planning can help to reduce any lack of clarity between roles and responsibilities; it sets clear boundaries about who is responsible for what will happen in the session and when; about how the session will be delivered; about the resources to be prepared and by whom; and it can also help to establish a good working relationship in the classroom between the teacher and TA which will in turn have a positive effect on the learner's experiences. Robert and the TA should sit down together and look at the aims and learning objectives for the session, and be explicit about the learning and assessment outcomes expected of Sophie. They should discuss and clarify how Robert is planning to deliver the session, the teaching strategies used, the learning and assessment tasks that are to be set, and when the different tasks are to be completed by Sophie. They need to agree the resources that Sophie will need to participate fully in the session and *fundamentally* who will provide them. Robert should provide the TA with a copy of the session plan for reference and they should agree that Robert will communicate regularly with Sophie and the TA during the session in case any additional guidance is needed about completing any of the learning or assessment tasks.
- Robert should encourage the TA to be proactive rather than reactive, to try to address situations as they arise and then to check with Robert that he is happy with the actions taken.
- Robert should speak to the LDDs co-ordinator about providing Sophie with a laptop.
- Robert, Sophie and the TA should have a three-way meeting at least once a term to discuss and resolve any ongoing issues.
- Robert should ensure that he is accessible to the TA via email or telephone, should she wish to discuss aspects of Sophie's progress with him.
- Robert might think about any continuing professional development that both the TA and he might benefit from undertaking.

In this chapter so far we have explored Dewey's and Schön's notions of reflective practice. Another model of reflective practice that is effective and easy to use is Brookfield's Critical Lenses (1986). Brookfield's lenses enable us to reflect critically upon our practice from four different perspectives. He calls these perspectives 'lenses' and they are as follows:

- our own perspective;
- the point of view of our learners;
- the point of view of our colleagues; and
- the point of view of established theory.

This is a useful and practical framework that can be used by teachers and trainers in the Lifelong Learning sector to evaluate incidents in practice in order to produce an action plan for positive change. Consider the following scenario, in which a trainee teacher, Marcus, inadvertently uses Brookfield's approach in order to analyse a difficult situation he has encountered in his practice. He only realises he has carried this out following a teacher-training session when models of reflective practice, including Brookfield, are being discussed. As you read the following Close Focus, try to identify where Marcus has applied the four lenses.

CLOSE FOCUS **CLOSE** FOCUS **CLOSE** FOCUS **CLOSE** FOCUS **CLOSE** FOCUS

Marcus is completing a review of his mid-year learner questionnaire feedback as part of the process of reviewing a programme of study that he has delivered for the first time. Although generally the data is positive, one or two areas have been highlighted that are of concern to Marcus. The first is that 25% of the students have identified that the resources they were provided with were not useful in supporting the outcomes of the session, and secondly, 20% of the students felt that the teaching and learning methods used were not useful to them. Marcus is aware that there is a forthcoming staff–student programme board and he decides to try to find out from the students what the issues have been so that he can plan for and improve his future practice.

At the programme board, Marcus is surprised by the feedback he receives. One student representative is one of the learners that gave negative comments about the two areas indicated. When he is asked if he is prepared to expand on the issues, the learner informs Marcus that he is happy to do so and informs Marcus that he has a specific learning difficulty with reading (dyslexia) and that on occasions the handouts that are provided are confusing. The learner also informs Marcus that he often delivers large amounts of content orally, and that he cannot take in such large amounts of information as he has short-term memory problems and issues with processing and retaining information. Following the meeting Marcus thinks about the issues that have been raised and decides to consult with his more experienced colleagues to see if they have any practical advice for him. At the same time, he decides that he needs to be more aware of the problems associated with the specific learning difficulty (dyslexia) and reads around the subject to increase his knowledge. Following these two activities Marcus thinks that he is in a position to address the needs of this particular learner and he arranges a tutorial to discuss what can be done for the remainder of the programme to support his individual needs. The outcome of this meeting is that Marcus will review the content of handouts to be provided to the learner. Marcus also decides that a positive way forward is to produce some materials for the VLE, such as narrated presentations, which he will place alongside the handouts (with key points highlighted) and further learning activities which are to be completed by the learner alongside the narrated presentation. This will enable the learner to go back over the content of the sessions as often as he needs to and repeat tasks until learning has taken place. Because of the reading Marcus has done he is conscious that by doing this he is providing opportunities for multi-sensory learning. The learner will be able to *see* the presentation, *hear* it, repeat sections back to himself (*say* it) and *feel* it (complete learning activities on a simultaneous basis). Multi-sensory approaches to teaching and learning are the most effective strategies that can be used to promote inclusion for learners with dyslexia (Lee, 2002). Marcus also realises that this will benefit all the students in the class and not just the one learner. Now Marcus is more aware of the issues the learner faces, he is more conscious of the way he delivers the content of the sessions and he tries to build in different strategies for presenting information, such as visual aids.

Did you identify where Marcus applied Brookfield's lenses?

Meeting the diverse needs of learners in Lifelong Learning settings is not easy. In summary, we would encourage constant reflection on practice and the use of a recognised model for this reflection to assist in this process. We hope that this chapter has provided not only some insights into the challenges faced in delivering inclusive teaching and learning sessions but has also provided some positive support and guidance as to how this can be made a reality.

A SUMMARY OF **KEY POINTS**

In this chapter we have:

> explored how being a reflective practitioner can assist you in the ongoing improvement of your teaching and learning practices;

> evaluated how adapting teaching and learning practices can have a positive impact on promoting inclusion;

> discussed how collaborative working can have a positive impact on your classroom practices.

REFERENCES AND FURTHER READING REFERENCES AND FURTHER READING

Books

Brookfield, S (1986) *Understanding and Facilitating Adult Learning*. Milton Keynes: Open University Press.

Dewey, J (1933) *How We Think*. Lexington, MA: Heath.

Lee, J (2002) *Making the Curriculum Work for Learners with Dyslexia*. London: Basic Skills Agency.

Schön, D (1983) *The Reflective Practitioner: how professionals think in action*. Aldershot: Ashgate.

Tomlinson, C A (1997) *Differentiation of Instruction in Mixed Ability Classrooms*. Idaho, USA: Idaho Council for Exceptional Children.

Wallace, S (ed.) (2010) *The Lifelong Learning Sector Reflective Reader*. Exeter: Learning Matters.

Journal articles

General Teaching Council for England (2007) Research for Teachers: Reflection-in-Action Reflection-on-Action (on-line http://www.gtce.org.uk/pdf/tla/rft/reflection0507)

Government publications

DfES (2000) *Supporting the Teaching Assistant: A good practice guide*. London: Crown Publications.

7
An inclusive curriculum

By the end of this chapter you should:

- understand the meaning and implications of an inclusive approach to curriculum planning;
- be developing a critical understanding of the role played by policy in shaping inclusive approaches to curriculum;
- understand the ways in which curricula documents provide a frame of reference for discussions about an inclusive curriculum.

Professional Standards

This chapter relates to the following Professional Standards:

Professional Values:

AS 3 Equality, diversity and inclusion in relation to learners, the workforce and the community.

Professional Knowledge and Understanding:

AK 3.1 Issues of equality, diversity and inclusion.

Professional Practice:

AP 3.1 Apply principles to evaluate and develop own practice in promoting equality and inclusive learning and engaging with diversity.

Introduction

What is an 'inclusive curriculum'? By now, the definitions and understandings of inclusion and inclusive practice that this book rests on have become quite clear. But curriculum is a term that we have yet to introduce into the current discussion, and is a somewhat ambiguous term. This book is not the place for a critical discussion about all the possible meanings of curriculum. But at the same time, some kind of working definition is needed. Sometimes 'curriculum' is used to define a subject or a topic: 'the electrical installation curriculum' or 'the hair and beauty' curriculum, for example. At other times, it is used when describing a broader area of study and work: 'the vocational curriculum' or 'the adult numeracy core curriculum'. When prefixed with a variety of other terms, education researchers use the word to analyse particular effects or consequences of educational provision: 'the hidden curriculum' and 'the total curriculum' are examples of this. It can also be used to describe the different ways in which an educational programme can be organised or sequenced, delivered as a 'spiral curriculum' or a 'thematic curriculum'. These – and other – terms or descriptors are commonly found in teacher-training textbooks and journal articles. As such, 'curriculum studies' is effectively a subject in itself, and one which can take us in all sorts of directions, ranging from practical issues such as how modules are timetabled, to pedagogical issues such as how different kinds of subjects should be taught and how they should be assessed. For the purposes of this discussion, we will limit our exploration of curriculum to the actual syllabuses or courses that are delivered within the Lifelong Learning sector, leaving broader issues such as funding mechanisms and political drivers to one side. And as before, our definition of inclusion encompasses all of those ways by which the provision of education and training can be made more accessible to any groups of potential students who might otherwise face structural, financial or cultural barriers to participation.

The inclusive curriculum: Starting at the top – the QCA

The Qualifications and Curriculum Authority (QCA) has been influential in planning and then enacting reforms for both young people and adults in relation not only to qualifications but also to the whole system within which qualifications are positioned. Over recent years, a number of significant changes have been introduced that can be seen as encouraging a more inclusive approach to curricula planning and provision. There are three key themes to consider in relation to provision within the Lifelong Learning sector: the 14–19 agenda; the implementation of functional skills within the curriculum; and the foundation learning tier.

New opportunities for the 14–19 age group, including Diplomas

From the outset, it is important to recognise that the changes that have been made to 14–19 provision during the last two years do not represent a pace of change that is new to the sector. Within both FE and adult education, new policy initiatives are rolled out on a frequent basis: indeed, some researchers have persuasively argued that practitioners are almost overwhelmed by the speed with which provision within the sector can change (Edward et al., 2007). At one level, therefore, the 14–19 Diplomas simply represent yet another example of a particular body of knowledge or skills that has been packaged and then delivered differently in comparison to previous academic years. Doing new things each academic year is, for most of us, not a surprise.

For some tutors in mainstream FE colleges, working with younger learners represents a more significant professional and personal challenge, and not solely because the QTLS curriculum is relatively quiet on the subject of 'working with 14–16s' (an expression invariably used by tutors and managers as a euphemism for managing classroom discipline). FE colleges have long been used to taking in the learners that nobody else wants or knows how to work with, and the 14–19 Agenda and the Diplomas are a natural extension of this, despite stereotypical complaints about FE colleges being used by schools as dumping grounds for the learners that they do not want to teach. By contrast, it would appear that for many young people, coming into FE does in fact represent a meaningful opportunity to learn and to work (Harkin, 2006). So what will Diplomas do differently, in comparison to existing qualifications and progression routes? There are two ways to think about this, both of which are relevant to an understanding of curricula as inclusive: firstly, we need to consider the implications for learning, teaching and assessment; secondly, we need to consider the logistical or practical consequences.

Learning, teaching and assessment

The Diploma model raises a number of interesting themes, although it is important to preface our discussion by remembering that to a large degree, Diplomas have absorbed and reworked, rather than rewritten, many existing qualification schemes. BTECs and A levels, for example, now form part of the Diploma structure, but are otherwise unchanged. Diplomas are structured in three parts:

1 Principal learning (which relates to the specific occupational area that the Diploma rests in).
2 Generic learning (including functional skills – which we shall return to shortly).
3 Additional learning (optional components that allow an element of Diploma personalisation).

Perhaps the most immediate aspects of Diploma provision as they relate to learning and teaching issues are the different learning and teaching environments that 14–16 students might be expected to participate in. The environment of a FE college is quite different from that of a school, and practitioners in the FE sector hold teaching qualifications that rarely, if at all, pay specific heed to learning and teaching issues as they affect younger learners. There is no mention of any specific pedagogies relating to 14–16 students within the QTLS framework. In addition, each Diploma has to include a work experience period of at least ten days in a 'real world environment', to provide students with a meaningful and authentic introduction to the world of work. But how will what is learned during these placements be recognised and rewarded? Is it sufficient to assume that the provision of more flexible, work-related courses will help increase motivation and achievement among learners, and hence widen participation?

Logistics and practicalities

At a practical level, the technicalities of establishing new forms of working relationships between schools, colleges and employers would not seem insurmountable. And it surely makes sense to expand the provision of vocational or craft-based curricula for students aged 14 or 15 who are disengaged, or at risk of disengaging, from mainstream education provision. Some of the logistical problems might not seem to have been thoroughly thought through: how these learners will travel to the different sites that deliver their learning is one important issue; how different schools and colleges will be able to synchronise their timetables is another. And as college tutors increasingly find themselves working with younger learners, issues of professional parity with schoolteachers, such as pay scales or teaching workloads, may begin to emerge. It is the extent of the Diploma's success in encouraging more young people to stay in education or training for longer, and to experience greater levels of progression and success as they do so that matters, and it will be some time before their success can be properly evaluated.

The functional skills approach, and the move away from key and basic skills

Since the publication of the Moser Report, *A Fresh Start: improving literacy and numeracy*, in 1999, the development of literacy and numeracy skills has been a central, and much-debated, component of provision within the learning and skills sector. Courses for younger learners at colleges, for work-based learners and for adults attending classes in community settings have benefited from new core curricula, new tranches of funding and newly qualified staff. And yet the nature of this provision continues to change and be changed. It seems that barely a year goes by without a new literacy or numeracy initiative being launched by the appropriate government department or agency, which themselves change name and focus with sometimes bewildering speed. Thus, many teachers and trainers in the Lifelong

Learning sector now find themselves delivering functional skills. These might be embedded within a GCSE or Diploma, or they might be delivered as a standalone qualification.

For a teacher or trainer committed to an inclusive approach to learning and teaching, this is an important issue. After all, what could be more important than helping our students gain those skills (whatever they might happen to be) that help them not only move into or through the world of work, but also move within and through society as a whole? Inclusion is about helping people gain the education that they need so that they can be economically independent. But it is also about helping people take a full part in the lives of their communities or their families. In a way, to describe these skills as 'functional' seems somewhat inadequate.

But what are functional skills? The QCA defines them as follows:

> *Functional skills are practical skills in English, Information and Communication Technology (ICT) and Mathematics, that allow individuals to work confidently, effectively and independently in life.*

Critics might indeed argue that the move from 'basic skills' to 'functional skills' is merely cosmetic. The 'basic skills' model was defined by the Basic Skills Agency as follows:

> *The ability to read, write and speak in English/Welsh and to use mathematics at a level necessary to function and progress at work and in society in general.*

The extent to which such a definition is satisfactory is open to question, however. Defining 'function' or 'functional' is perhaps more complex than it might at first appear, according to one of the more recent, substantial bodies of research that has been carried out regarding the provision of education and training for 14–19 year-olds:

> *Function must be defined in terms of that for which it is said to be functional, and that requires a detailed analysis of the job or mode of living for which the skills are needed.*
>
> (Pring et al., 2009, page 110)

So if functional skills are in some way related to the context within which they are to be used, then we might reasonably argue that the functional skills required by, for example, a plumber, would be different to those required by a beauty therapist. To the tutors working within these areas, this would probably not come as much of a surprise. But this poses a problem for tutors. Who assesses functional skills? Do literacy and numeracy specialists, holding specific literacy or numeracy qualifications, have the kinds of expertise or understanding of the functional skills needs of different occupational sectors, or will a more generic approach to functional skills become apparent?

The introduction of the foundation learning tier

At the time of writing this book, it was announced that 938,000 – 15.6% – of young people aged between 16 and 24 are classified as being not in employment, education or training (NEET), although among 16–18 year-olds the proportion of NEETs was put at the lower number of 8.5% (162,000), perhaps reflecting recent moves to increase the age at which young people are required to stay within formal education or training. In this context, any initiatives to allow curricula to be delivered in such a way that they can encourage a greater uptake from young people must therefore be seen as a good example of inclusive practice.

The recent changes to the organisation of qualifications structures that led to the establishment of the Qualifications and Curriculum Framework (QCF) also served to pave the way for an approach to planning for learning that can rest on more personalised routes or schemes. That is to say, if as a consequence of broader reform of vocational qualifications (in itself no bad thing – the range and variety of vocational and technical qualifications continues to be bewildering), the focus of curricular planning considers not only whole programmes but also how individual *units* fit within these, then perhaps these units could be combined in new and innovative ways – perhaps in ways that the authors of the curricula did not originally consider – to create different, personalised programmes of study.

This is the central idea that currently underpins *foundation learning*. The foundation learning tier is the term used to describe all provision at both entry level and level 1 on the QCF. It is organised to meet the needs of both 14–19 learners and adults (who are here described as being aged over 19), and was originally envisaged to be fully in place by 2013 (although the change in government in 2010 leaves things far from certain). The idea behind the foundation learning tier is that, alongside existing curricula schemes such as apprenticeships, this more flexible scheme can provide 'destination-led' qualifications to learners currently working at entry level or level 1 to help them progress to a level 2 award that in turn will lead to greater employment chances. And so there are three components to the scheme: a subject area or vocational area component; a functional skills component that incorporates literacy, numeracy and ICT; and a personal and social development component.

The scheme is geared towards three main cohorts. Firstly, it is designed for those young people who are either NEET, or at risk of becoming so: indeed, a reduction in the number of people who are classed as NEET is a major aim of this initiative, according to the Learning and Skills Information Service (LSIS). Secondly, it is designed for young people who have not achieved five good GCSE passes. And thirdly, it is designed for students who have specific needs, or who have SpLDs. But it is important to state that this provision does not intend to be the *only* curriculum available to these three groups. Rather, it is designed in such a way that people within those groups – who are at a greater-than-average risk of dropping out of formal education or training without good qualifications – can be encouraged to stay and can have schemes designed for them that will meet their individual needs. As such, the construction of the foundation learning tier rests on *personalised learning*, framed within an individual learning plan – a common feature of adult basic education for many years, and increasingly used throughout both the FE and HE sectors. Potential students will begin their journey through the programme with an initial assessment and an induction, at which any relevant previous experience that they might have can be accredited through an Accreditation of Prior Experiential Learning (APEL) process, thereby quickly giving students some kind of formal certification. After this, the exact shape of the student's portfolio will be negotiated with their advisers and/or tutors, in order to take into account their specialist area, their functional skills needs, and their personal and social development.

Summing up

Thus far, we have looked at three main strands of curriculum reform or provision that can be seen as encouraging inclusive practice: the 14–19 agenda; functional skills; and foundation learning. These three are of course all inter-related. The move to functional skills has been carried out as part of a broader reform of the 14–19 curriculum, and in turn makes up a significant component of the foundation learning tier. Similarly, the establishment of the QCF, as part of this broader reform, has helped establish the unit-based credit framework that makes personalised learning for foundation tier students practicable and achievable. So what might the impact of such reforms be? Overall, it could be argued that they all share a single overall ambition: to increase participation in formal education or training (whether full-time or part-time) among those sectors of society who are currently under-represented. SEN students are included in this: but how successfully do colleges *currently* manage students with specific needs, whether these are physical disabilities, or social and emotional difficulties?

RESEARCH FOCUS RESEARCH FOCUS RESEARCH FOCUS RESEARCH FOCUS RESEARCH FOCUS

14–16 provision within mainstream FE: the challenges of SEBD

SEBD stands for social, emotional and behavioural difficulties. It is a problematic term, but tends to be used to describe and explain persistent disruptive behaviour, social problems or emotional difficulties that lead to the impairment of learning. Such behaviours are defined as persistent, but not necessarily permanent. In a research article published in 2008, *Provision in Further Education Colleges for 14- to 16-year-olds with Social, Emotional and Behavioural Difficulties* by Natasha Macnab, John Visser and Harry Daniels, a number of issues regarding the engagement of such students within FE are discussed. Based on the findings of their research from across ten FE colleges, the authors concluded that FE teaching staff were on the whole positive about working with younger students, but that more professional development was needed in order to equip teachers with the professional knowledge that they would need. And it is important to note that this positivity was not affected by either the 'challenges' that SEBD students bring to class, or the fact that for some of these young people, enrolment at a FE college was used by other agencies – schools, in particular – as an 'easy option' for managing 'unwanted' young people.

Consider these issues in the light of your own professional experiences as a tutor. Are groups of students such as those described above present within the FE college where you work or where you are on placement? Do you teach students such as these, and do you consider that you have received, or are about to receive, appropriate professional training and support?

The inclusive curriculum: a case study of a single programme

Up to this point, this chapter has looked at quite broad curricular initiatives that are designed to encourage an inclusive approach to participation in learning. In Chapter 6, by contrast, we explored a number of aspects of classroom practice from an inclusive perspective, by focusing on how we, as teachers and trainers, respond to students with dyslexia or to students who are visually impaired. As such, it seems appropriate to explore the ground that exists between these two points, between sector-wide reform and the practice of an individual teacher in their classroom. That is to say, it seems appropriate to explore the ways in which a curriculum, defined as a programme of study, might be seen as inclusive.

Case Study: NCFE level 2 Certificate in Counselling Skills

In the preceding chapter, we explored a case study based around a counselling skills tutor, Stuart, who had to plan and make adjustments for two of his students who each presented with quite different needs: one student is hearing impaired, and the other has dyslexia. In the case study, we learned that Stuart was not this group's regular tutor, and he was in some ways unprepared for working with the group. In the end, he coped with the needs of his students rather well. By returning to the level 2 counselling course in the context of this chapter, we can begin to look at the ways in which inclusive practice can be planned for across programmes of study, rather than 'just' in the classroom. There are two elements to consider here: firstly, the ways in which the course tutor (as distinct from a colleague who has been asked to cover at the last minute) anticipates and records responses to the needs of the students; and secondly, the ways in which the course is actually constructed to allow for specific student needs to be accounted for with a minimum of fuss or delay.

Implementing an inclusive programme of study

There's a lot of paperwork involved in being a teacher or trainer in the Lifelong Learning sector. Individual learning plans, schemes of work, tracking sheets, handouts – documents such as these shape our working lives in all kinds of ways. Lesson plans are a good example. In reality, and despite what teacher-training students get told in their CertEd/PGCE or DTLLS classes, the vast majority of teachers only write lesson plans when they are being observed (by an Ofsted inspector, a college quality-assurance manager or even their teacher-training lecturer). This is not to say that teachers do not actually plan their sessions, but there is a difference between the action of lesson planning and the action of writing up a lesson plan. Writing lesson plans can take a lot of time (Sharon and Jonathan continue to be somewhat amazed by the detailed minutiae that some college lesson plan templates ask for): if you teach in two-hour blocks, you might be expected to deliver twelve or thirteen separate sessions each week. That's a lot of lesson plans.

But if Stuart had been given a copy of a detailed lesson plan in advance of the counselling class, imagine how much more straightforward things would have been. Specific sections or boxes for differentiation, inclusive practice or SEN are frequently included on lesson plans. If the course tutor had drawn up their lesson plans in advance, with appropriate notes about the needs of the student with a hearing impairment and the student with dyslexia, then Stuart would have been able to reflect on possible changes to his teaching style before the class, rather than having to react to those students' discomfiture during the session. Writing lesson plans, therefore, need not only be about keeping observers and inspectors happy. It can also help create a support network for other tutors who may have to step in.

To be fair, writing reams of lesson plans one, two or three weeks before the lesson in question is actually going to be taught, might be seen as premature. Teachers in the Lifelong Learning sector need to be reflexive and responsive, taking account of how a session goes before planning what they will do next time. If students find a particular topic difficult, then teachers may need to spend longer on it. One of the units that make up the Certificate in Counselling Skills is called Diversity and Ethics in the Use of Counselling Skills, a potentially tricky subject that might require longer to discuss than first anticipated. Many teachers who do write lesson plans, therefore, tend to complete them more-or-less immediately prior to the session itself. So, if Stuart is not going to be given a lesson plan to work with when covering the counselling class, what other documentation might the course tutor have prepared?

Arguably, writing lesson plans is not that helpful for much of the time. But writing schemes of work and keeping an up-to-date tracking file for each group of students is useful and valuable. Schemes of work, if done properly, can include both the outline topics for each session and links to relevant curriculum documentation (to which we shall return shortly), and these can nearly always be downloaded from the awarding body's website. As such, if a substitute tutor, like Stuart, is asked to cover at a late stage, he can quickly find out what the students are doing that week, how it relates to the unit they are working on, and where this unit fits into the overall curriculum scheme. And a tracking file, containing notes about attendance and progression, assessment completion rates, diagnostic assessment results, copies of statements from educational psychologists or the outcomes from disability assessments, could have helped Stuart get to know the counselling group in advance of actually teaching the session.

We started this section by considering the sheer volume of paperwork that tutors have to deal with. And quite frankly, much of it gets in the way. But some of it is both useful and important, and we would argue that creating a paper-based *course file* for each module or unit that you teach, consisting of a detailed scheme of work and relevant tracking information, is a good thing to do. This is not just because it will help your colleagues cover your sessions for you if you are absent due to illness or another unforeseen event (although it will, of course), but because the act of planning across a unit or module as a whole will help you focus on what is needed to ensure that the unit is inclusive, whether this means accounting for SEN statements, adjusting assessment deadlines, rearranging room layouts or making space for learning support workers.

Constructing an inclusive programme of study

Much of the work in planning for an inclusive unit or programme of study is down to the individual teacher or trainer, therefore. If Stuart was to be given leadership of the level 2 counselling course, creating a detailed course file might well be one of the first jobs he would complete, bearing in mind his previous experiences of being in at the deep end. In doing so, he would be able to draw on the expertise of other specialist members of staff within his own institution. But he would also have to be thoroughly acquainted with those aspects of the course curriculum that impact on inclusive practice. So when designing his scheme of work, when timetabling the assessment schedule and when thinking about, for example, what kinds of adjustments he is allowed to make to help a student who is hearing-impaired, or who has dyslexia, Stuart would need to refer at first to the awarding body's own policies or regulations, as well as to the curriculum specifications that the awarding body has published. That is to say, the extent to which this counselling curriculum (or any other programme of study) can be seen as being inclusive rests in part on how the curriculum is specified by the awarding body, as well as how it is experienced by tutors and students.

PRACTICAL TASK PRACTICAL TASK PRACTICAL TASK PRACTICAL TASK PRACTICAL TASK

Before reading on, it would be helpful for you to download two pdf documents from the NCFE website: firstly, the curriculum specifications for the level 2 Certificate in Counselling Skills; and secondly, the NCFE Reasonable Adjustments and Special Considerations Policy. As is the case with documentation produced by many other awarding bodies (such as NOCN or Ascentis), curriculum specifications are freely available from their websites. Spend some time familiarising yourself with the documents, and reflect on how they are organised and what information and guidance they contain that might have an impact on the inclusivity (in the widest sense) of the curriculum that they specify.

The curriculum documentation for the NCFE level 2 Certificate in Counselling Skills contains all of the features that we would expect to see, such as:

- the aims and objectives of the qualification;
- mapping to relevant national occupational standards;
- how the qualification is assessed and moderated, including how each unit might be assessed;
- unit summaries that include details such as guided learning hours and credit values for each unit.

As well as these, however, there are also some details that demonstrate an inclusive ethos at work:

Entry guidance

This course has no specified prior learning requirements and admissions decisions are made at the discretion of the college where the course is being run. This allows admissions tutors an excellent level of flexibility in deciding who can come on the course, and will allow them to take all kinds of individual considerations into account.

Credit accumulation and transfer

Because students gain credit for each individual unit that they study within the QCF, these credits can be imported into any new relevant programme of study that the student might enrol on. In this way, if a student has to leave or transfer out from a programme of study, they will be able to take the credits that they have already earned and put them towards a new qualification. Moreover, the use of APL (referred to within this curriculum scheme as the Recognition of Prior Learning – RPL) allows candidates to gain exemption from studying a unit if they can demonstrate relevant prior experience or learning, for which they can receive certification.

The Candidate Learning Log (CLL)

The CLL is the template that NCFE provide for candidates to use when building their assessment portfolios. It is downloadable – free of charge – from the NCFE website. But if students so wish, and tutors agree, they are free to use any method of their own choosing when compiling their portfolios.

Up to this point, it would seem to be the case that this qualification has indeed been designed with an inclusive ethos at its centre: entry routes are highly flexible; assessment methods can be tailored to suit the individual; and students can travel between this and other qualifications if their circumstances change. But NCFE go further, and also provide additional guidance in the form of a Reasonable Adjustments and Special Considerations Policy. This policy, which the CLL refers to, has a number of important features:

Reasonable adjustment

Reasonable adjustments are those measures that can be taken to allow students who have either a permanent or temporary disability or other impairment, to complete the assessment for the course in such a way that the assessment is still both valid and reliable. Commonly used techniques or strategies that would be classified as 'reasonable adjustments' include:

- the provision of a note-taker or BSL interpreter;
- providing alternative accommodation for a closed examination;
- allowing additional time for a student to complete a piece of work;
- allowing a candidate to use assistive ICT.

Special considerations

If a student feels that, due to a temporary or unforeseen circumstance (for example, a family bereavement), they have under-performed in an assessment, they can ask for this to be taken into account during the marking and moderation process. In these special circumstances, it may be decided that the student's marks might be adjusted; it might even be decided that the student be allowed to resubmit the assessment; or it might be decided that no adjustment is to be made because to do so would unduly favour the student. At all times, the overall validity and reliability of the assessment process would need to be maintained.

Case study: NCFE level 2 Certificate in Counselling Skills – summing up

If Stuart is going to become the new course leader for the counselling course, he should have no major problems in designing an inclusive curriculum, from the moment when a student is enrolled to the moment when a student completes their assessments. The curriculum documentation sets out a number of policies or frameworks that can inform Stuart's planning. And if Stuart does get stuck – after all, he is not a SEN or disability specialist, nor is he expected to become one – he will be able to look for help from the college SEN adviser or the awarding body's quality-assurance team.

Conclusion

As teachers and trainers, our planning and designing for inclusive practice needs to take into account not only those individual sessions that we teach in our workshops and classrooms, but also the way in which the entirety of the courses or curricula that we teach are planned and prepared for. When planning for inclusion, therefore, we need to start to think about how to make our lessons, our assessments, even our programmes of study as inclusive as they can possibly be, while still maintaining the rigour and quality of the provision. Awarding bodies help create a framework for this, but it is down to us to make it happen.

A SUMMARY OF **KEY POINTS**

In this chapter we have looked at the following key points:

> **how we define and understand the term 'inclusive curriculum';**

> **the role of the QCA in enabling an inclusive curriculum through curricula reform, the 14–19 Agenda and the implementation of the foundation learning tier;**

> **working with 14–16 students in FE colleges, and the particular challenges posed by SEBD;**

> **working with curriculum specifications and interpreting policies and procedures established by awarding bodies.**

REFERENCES AND FURTHER READING REFERENCES AND FURTHER READING

Books

Peart, S and Atkins, L (2011) *Teaching 14–19 Learners in the Lifelong Learning Sector*. Exeter: Learning Matters.

Pring, R, Hayward, G, Hodgson, A, Johnson, J, Keep, E, Oancea, A, Rees, G, Spours, K and Wilde, S (2009) *Education for All: the future of education and training for 14–19 year olds.* London: Routledge.

Journal articles

Edward, S, Coffield, F, Steer, R and Gregson, M (2007) Endless change in the learning and skills sector: the impact on teaching staff. *Journal of Vocational Education and Training*, 59(2): 155–73.

Harkin, J (2006) Treated like adults: 14–16 year-olds in further education. *Research in Post-Compulsory Education*, 11(3): 319–39.

Macnab, N, Visser, J and Daniels, H (2008) Provision in Further Education colleges for 14 to 16-year-olds with social, emotional and behavioural difficulties. *British Journal of Special Education*, 35(4): 241–46.

Websites

Ofqual – the Office of Qualifications and Examinations Regulation: the QCF framework is discussed at: www.ofqual.gov.uk/qualification-and-assessment-framework/89-articles/145-explaining-the-qualifications-and-credit-framework

NCFE – the level 2 Certificate in Counselling Skills course can be downloaded from: www.ncfe.org.uk/Home.aspx

8
Inclusive policies and inclusive practice

By the end of this chapter you should:

- have a developing understanding of the relationship between education policy and education practice, as it relates to inclusion in education;
- be aware of the main aspects of the 2010 Equality Act that relate to provision within the Lifelong Learning sector.

Professional Standards

This chapter relates to the following Professional Standards:

Professional Values:

AS 3 Equality, diversity and inclusion in relation to learners, the workforce and the community.

Professional Knowledge and Understanding:

AK 3.1 Issues of equality, diversity and inclusion.

FK 1.1 Sources of information, advice, guidance and support to which learners might be referred.

FK 1.2 Internal services which learners might access.

Professional Practice:

AP 3.1 Apply principles to evaluate and develop own practice in promoting equality and inclusive learning and engaging with diversity.

B 1.2 Establish and maintain procedures with learners which promote and maintain appropriate behaviour, communication and respect for others, while challenging discriminatory behaviours and attitudes.

Introduction

During the course of this book, we have explored a number of authentic case studies that show how meeting a student who uses a wheelchair, or a student who is accompanied by a sign language interpreter, or a student who has another member of college staff helping them on a one-to-one basis throughout the college day, is an increasingly common occurrence within the Lifelong Learning sector. It is no longer acceptable practice (as it once was, not all that long ago) for students with disabilities to be excluded from mainstream educational opportunities and instead be restricted to education in special schools and colleges. Ways can be found of accommodating students with disabilities in colleges, partly thanks to technology, and partly thanks to the changing attitudes of society at large. Changing social attitudes can be seen as both shaping and being shaped by changes in legislation that now mean, among many other things, that it is illegal for providers of education and training to discriminate against a student on the basis of, for example, disability.

Over the last 30 years or so, successive governments have made more or less profound changes to educational systems and structures at sometimes bewildering speed. Indeed, as we were at the very last stages of writing this book, Michael Gove, Secretary of State for Education, announced the publication of a government inquiry, led by Professor Alison Wolf, into the provision of vocational and technical qualifications. If all of the Wolf Report's conclusions are accepted, then the nature of the 14–19 curriculum, and the specific qualifications schemes that are currently found within it, look set to change again – in some ways quite drastically – only three years after the implementation of the previous government's changes to the same area of provision. As soon as the report was published, Michael Gove announced that the following recommendations were to be implemented immediately:

1   Qualified FE lecturers (that is, lecturers who have achieved QTLS through the professional formation process) would be allowed to teach in school classrooms on the same basis as qualified schoolteachers.
2   Rules on allowing industry professionals to teach in schools would be clarified, to make the process more straightforward.
3   Any vocational qualification offered by a regulated awarding body would be opened up for 14 to 19 year-olds.
4   Established high-quality vocational qualifications that have not been accredited within the QCF will be offered in schools and colleges from September 2011.

Not all of the recommendations made by the report were accepted at once. This is hardly surprising, as some of them will require considerable changes to existing curricular and financial structures within the Lifelong Learning sector. The report casts doubt on the future of the Diploma (which, as the report points out, has had a very low take-up rate of only 1% of the target population). Many other qualifications that are seen as leading students to a 'dead-end', with no meaningful hope of employment or future education or training, are also likely to come under review. Clearly another period of change may well be round the corner. But two of Wolf's further recommendations are of real importance to the specific issues in this book. They are:

1   14 to 16 year-olds should be allowed to enrol in colleges so they can benefit from the high-quality vocational training that is available within the sector.
2   Anyone who fails to get a good pass (a C grade or above) in GCSE English or Mathematics must continue to study those subjects post-16.

It goes without saying that education is a big subject for politicians, not least because so much public money gets spent on it. The depth of political engagement with education has, arguably, deepened during the past 30 years or so, a process that can be seen as beginning with the implementation in 1988 of the National Curriculum by the then Secretary of State for Education, Kenneth Baker. Education researchers and philosophers have differing points of view about the extent to which the state should – or should not – intervene in educational provision. Indeed, another of Michael Gove's policies – free schools – would seem to indicate that the current government is, in some areas at least, seeking to reduce its educational footprint. But without the specific force of legislation, would our education systems be as inclusive as they are? We have already argued that social attitudes towards people with learning difficulties, or people who have either seen or unseen disabilities, have changed for the better. But without the 1981 Education Act which implemented the Warnock Report of 1978, or the 2001 Special Needs and Disability Act which paved the way for the new Special Educational Needs code of practice the following year, would FE colleges and adult education providers be working as much as they currently do to enable an inclusive learning environment?

Education and policy: some introductory comments

It was in 1870 that education first came under the purview of government, with the passing of the first Education Act. Children were to be taught reading, writing and arithmetic and religious instruction, and until 30 years later, teachers received payment according to results. If children failed their tests, then this proved that they had not been taught properly. Provision for students with learning difficulties or disabilities, meanwhile, first attracted government legislation in 1893, when the Elementary Education (Blind and Deaf Children) Act was passed, and again in 1899, when the Elementary Education (Defective and Epileptic Children) Act was passed. At this stage, as we noted in Chapter 2, decisions about the education of such children were still made by members of the medical profession, reflecting the medical model of disability that was dominant throughout much of the twentieth century.

The Warnock Report of 1978 led to the 1981 Education Act (also referred to in Chapter 2), which can be seen as the first of a series of important pieces of legislation relating to education and training as they impact on students with LDDs, or students who otherwise might be at risk of exclusion for either social or economic reasons. For the purposes of our discussion, we will look briefly at just four of these, before going on to explore more recent legislation – the 2010 Equality Act – that has served to gather together all previous anti-discriminatory legislation in one place.

The 1981 Education Act

In Chapter 2, some of the key recommendations of the 1978 Warnock Report were discussed. Arguably, three over-riding themes emerged from the report that are of particular relevance here. The first of these was the recommendation that as far as possible, SEN students should be educated within mainstream settings. The second of these was the finding that young people themselves felt anger at being excluded from mainstream education, which in turn led to a broader sense of social isolation. And thirdly, of particular relevance to the professional contexts within which this book is situated, the Report recommended that these same policies of inclusion be extended to the FE sector.

Many of the recommendations of the Warnock Report found their way into the 1981 Education Act, which required LEAs to provide appropriate diagnostic assessment for children with SEN. The ways in which these educational needs would be met were to be written up in a *statement* that would, in effect, accompany the child as they travelled through the education system. What the Act did not do, however, was provide any definition of what SEN might actually be, other than:

> *A child has special educational needs if he has a learning difficulty which calls for special educational provision to be made for him [sic].*

The 1994 Special Needs Code of Practice

One of the criticisms of the 1988 National Curriculum was that it made schools unwilling to work with children who had SEN or disabilities. Because the testing and assessment regime that the National Curriculum introduced was based on levels of attainment according to age, and because test results were used to indicate the effectiveness of a school, schools became unwilling to accommodate those children who might be unable to achieve these goals. Six years later, however, the 1994 Special Needs Code of Practice was introduced. This was a significant act, and not only because it was based on a social rather than a medical model of disability. The Code also defined eight different kinds of SEN:

I   Learning difficulties
II   Specific learning difficulties
III   Emotional and behavioural difficulties
IV   Physical disabilities
V   Visual impairments
VI   Hearing impairments
VII   Speech impairments
VIII Medical conditions

The 2001 Special Needs and Disability Act

The 2001 Special Needs and Disability Act was introduced in part to meet criticisms of the 1994 Code, which was seen by some as overly bureaucratic, and so some of the procedures of the earlier Code were streamlined (such as rewording the list of kinds of educational need so that the number of categories could be halved, and so that fewer targets were set). A more significant aspect of the 2001 Act was the enhancement of the rights of children and parents to be involved in those target setting and planning processes that had previously been under the control of education professionals.

The 2002 Disability Discrimination Act (part four)

The Disability Discrimination Act was introduced in 1995. In 2002, part four of the Act was published, which extended the scope of the original legislation to include education providers. According to the DDA part four, discrimination against a student might come about in two ways:

- failing to make 'reasonable adjustment' for a student with a disability;
- treating a student with a disability 'less favourably' for a reason related *to that disability*.

In addition, educational institutions also became legally obliged to:

- raise staff awareness relating to working with students with disabilities;
- be proactive in assessing and responding to individuals' disabilities.

The 2010 Equality Act

Different pieces of legislation that have served to outlaw particular kinds of discriminatory behaviour (such as the Race Relations Act or the Equal Pay Act) date back 40 years. In 2010, the then Labour government introduced a single piece of legislation that was designed to both encompass all pre-existing anti-discriminatory behaviour and also ensure that any discrepancies that had existed between different earlier statutes were reconciled. Consequently, the Equality Act is a comprehensive and lengthy piece of legislation. Part six, chapter two of the Act relates to the provision of education and training by FE and HE institutions.

The terms of the Equality Act impact on all aspects of the educational provision offered by FE providers, and it outlaws discriminatory or unfavourable treatment from the point of enrolment to the point of qualification and beyond. The Act requires all FE providers (which include not only colleges but also private training providers, or indeed any organisation that offers any formal provision that is endorsed by an appropriate body) to make *reasonable adjustments* so that discriminatory treatment is avoided. Such adjustments may relate to the ways in which actual courses or modules are delivered, but they may also relate to wider services provided by the college, such as financial help or counselling services. That is to say, *all* of the different aspects of the FE curriculum (courses, support services, accommodation and so on) are subject to the Act. In addition, colleges need to ensure that they provide equality of access and service for all students, irrespective of whether or not they have a disability (that may or may not have been disclosed by the individual), and for any other people who may have access to college facilities but who are not actually enrolled as students within that institution – for example, members of the public who use college sports halls to play five-a-side football.

The 2010 Equality Act close-up

Reading the entire text of the Equality Act is probably not necessary for most teachers and trainers in the learning and skills sector. Part six chapter two, though, is relatively short and straightforward. A link to the full text can be found at the end of this chapter. Here we will focus on just three short extracts from the Act.

First extract
> (1) *The responsible body of an institution to which this section applies must not discriminate against a person–*
> (a) *in the arrangements it makes for deciding who is offered admission as a student;*
> (b) *as to the terms on which it offers to admit the person as a student;*
> (c) *by not admitting the person as a student.*

This first part of the Act relates to any individual person who may wish to enrol on either a programme of study or an individual module or unit: the same conditions apply, irrespective of the size or length of the course or programme being applied to. Quite simply, it means that it is illegal to discriminate against a prospective student during the admissions process either by changing the ways in which enrolment is performed, changing the criteria that are used for enrolment or simply not allowing a student to enrol.

Implications for practice
This does not mean, however, that admissions systems all have to be regulated and policed; nor does it mean that any discretionary aspects of the admissions process that tutors can and do use need to be put to one side. It is still perfectly possible – and lawful – to admit a number of students to a programme of study even if these students all have quite different entry qualifications and if some of them are going through an APEL process. But if some aspect of the admissions or enrolment process had the effect of disadvantaging somebody on the basis of a disability, or on cultural grounds, then that would be unlawful. For example, if a tutor decided to hold a compulsory pre-enrolment session on the same day that a

religious holiday fell, then it would be illegal for the tutor to subsequently exclude any student who could not attend the session that day because they were engaged in their religious observances. It would also be discriminatory if an admissions tutor prevented an applicant with a physical impairment from enrolling on a science course. Instead, the applicant should be allowed to enrol, assuming they meet the entry criteria for the course (including taking into account any flexibility or discretion that the curriculum allows for). After this, the college then needs to make appropriate and reasonable adjustments so that the student can take part. This might involve rearranging furniture, changing room layouts and altering assessment procedures (with the approval of the awarding body).

Second extract

> (2) The responsible body of such an institution must not discriminate against a student–
> (a) in the way it provides education for the student;
> (b) in the way it affords the student access to a benefit, facility or service;
> (c) by not providing education for the student;
> (d) by not affording the student access to a benefit, facility or service;
> (e) by excluding the student;
> (f) by subjecting the student to any other detriment.

This part of the Act relates to students once they have actually enrolled at the institution. It states that the institution (which might be a FE college, a private training provider, a work-based learning provider or an adult education institution) must not discriminate against its students in the provision of education, or of any other service or facility.

Implications for practice

Once a student has actually enrolled at a college, therefore, all aspects of the student's experience become subject to this legislation. What happens within the workshop or classroom is covered by the Act; so is what happens in the library or the computer lab, the canteen or the Students' Union. Earlier chapters in this book contain examples both of potentially discriminatory practices, and responses to them. In Chapter 2, we followed David, a full-time teacher-training student, on placement and learned that he was surprised to encounter a deaf student in his level 3 class. The case study in Chapter 6 when Stuart was teaching a level 2 counselling class on behalf of a colleague detailed his responses to the specific needs of two further students (one with dyslexia and one with a hearing impairment). If these three students had repeatedly found themselves unable to participate fully in classes or assignments, then they could argue that they were being discriminated against. And it is important to recognise that these would be examples of discriminatory behaviour even if the tutor were not at all knowledgeable or experienced in managing such situations.

Third extract

> (8) The responsible body of such an institution must not victimise a disabled person–
> (a) in the arrangements it makes for deciding upon whom to confer a qualification;
> (b) as to the terms on which it is prepared to confer a qualification on the person;
> (c) by not conferring a qualification on the person;
> (d) by withdrawing a qualification from the person or varying the terms on which the person holds it.

Throughout those sections of the Act that deal with FE and HE institutions, there are some sections that address discriminatory behaviour against 'everyone', and other sections that address discriminatory behaviour against disabled people specifically. This is because it is not just people who are registered as having a disability who might be discriminated against – the legislation covers all forms of discrimination, after all. Nonetheless, some sections do deal specifically with disabled people, as this example shows. Here, the Act states that it is illegal to victimise a disabled person by treating them differently to an 'able-bodied' person (whatever that might mean) when actually awarding qualifications or certificates.

Implications for practice

For most of us, as teachers and trainers, decisions about accreditation or certification are only very rarely a part of our professional lives. Our involvement ends once we have completed our mark sheets and passed them on for second marking, or internal and external validation. That said, it is important for us to recognise that for anybody who is enrolled on a course or programme of study that we teach, the eventual award or qualification will always be the same. A foundation degree awarded to a student with a disability is 'the same' as a foundation degree awarded to anybody else.

The 2010 Equality Act – summing up

At its core, this new legislation does not in itself 'change' anything. All of the things that previous legislation such as DDA part four or SENDA talked about still apply. As such, all the training days and continuing professional development (CPD) events that we have (sometimes grudgingly) attended in the past are still relevant as we write this book. For some people, discussions of this kind lead to comments about 'political correctness', but to follow such a line of argument misses the point. Yes, we – tutors, course leaders, admissions tutors and college managers – are all required to act in an inclusive manner and to avoid discriminatory behaviour. But the adjustments that we are required to make only ever need to be *reasonable*. What is reasonable within a large mixed FE college might not be so for a small adult education provider. What is reasonable for a student on an access to the social sciences course may not be so for a student on a BTEC level 2 first certificate in applied science. And this is why, if there is ever any doubt as to what would be the best course of action to take, our first response as tutors should always be to consider who else, either in our institution or at the organisation which endorses the programmes we teach, we can talk to so that we might obtain advice which is both consistent and sound.

RESEARCH FOCUS RESEARCH FOCUS **RESEARCH FOCUS** RESEARCH FOCUS **RESEARCH FOCUS**

Reflecting on research and practice

For many tutors, one of the more difficult aspects of inclusive practice is in working with students with mental health issues. In a research article titled *Supporting Mental Health and Emotional Well-being among Younger Students in Further Education*, Warwick et al. reported on research that they had conducted at five different FE colleges, that provided mental health support services to students. The findings of the research can be grouped into six categories:

1 The FE sector

According to the authors, students within the FE sector are particularly prone to experiencing mental health issues for two reasons. Firstly, colleges are often used as a 'last chance' alternative to exclusion from mainstream education. Secondly, FE colleges (as distinct from sixth form colleges) are more likely to recruit students from areas that are *relatively* socially or economically deprived, which in turn may impact on the mental health of students from these areas.

2 Identification of needs

Within colleges, patterns of behaviour that might warrant a diagnosis in terms of mental health are often not seen as such. This is because for many college staff, such behaviour (such as being disruptive in class) is interpreted as being 'bad behaviour', and not a consequence of a mental health issue, which staff view as being something that affects adults, not younger people.

3 Leadership and management

As is the case in many other areas, so it is the case that the quality of college leadership is very variable in terms of planning for and responding to mental health concerns. This can lead to confusion for teaching staff who may lack clear policies or guidelines to work within.

4 Internal support services

A range of services is provided within FE colleges to provide mental health support for students. These range from the provision of learning support and personal tuition to the provision of special procedures for assessments and examinations, and counselling services.

5 External support services

Within the colleges where this research was conducted, much less use was made of support services provided by external organisations such as LEAs or charities. The article concludes that much more systematic use of such organisations can only be beneficial to the sector.

6 CPD for staff

And finally, the article notes that although time is precious and motivation might be low, additional staff training relating to issues such as self-harm or eating disorders needs to be rolled out to greater numbers of staff. As with disability and inclusive legislation more generally, this is not because all FE teachers and trainers need to be experts at helping students who self-harm. But if more tutors know what signs to look for, if more tutors are *sensitive* to the issue, then expert help can be found when it is needed.

Indeed, many of the issues that this article raises in relation to mental health are equally applicable to other inclusive practice themes. We cannot anticipate everything, nor can we be expected to know all of the answers all of the time. But if we know enough to help out in the first instance, and know who to refer students to for more in-depth support, and if we know enough to plan and organise our sessions in such a way that they are inclusive, then we can be confident that we are behaving appropriately and professionally.

REFLECTIVE TASK

Sitting an exam

Edward has worked as an adult education tutor since 1995, teaching a range of history classes. Until a couple of years ago, he taught history classes to adult learners at a large city-based university. Students on these programmes were 'typical' mature students – they had often left school aged 15 or 16, and had decided to return to learning later in life, often prompted either by changes to their employment status or to their family lives. History was a popular choice at the university's adult education centre: inspired by television programmes such as *Time Team* or *Who Do You Think You Are?*, many students found themselves wanting to learn more. The vast majority of the courses were assessed through coursework, but one of the modules (which was compulsory for students who wanted to gain their Certificate in History Studies) included a 'traditional' three-hour closed exam. In this excerpt from his reflective journal, Edward thinks back to the first time he taught the compulsory module.

I was aware from the very beginning of the term that this module would be tricky for some of the group. Not because of the course content – I was more than confident that I knew the subject well and also that I knew how to repackage and deliver that subject in such a way that the group would all be able to get to grips with it. There were plenty of books in the centre library, and all of my handouts were clear and easy to follow. But the assessment for the module was based on a 50-50 split between a coursework essay and a closed exam. The rationale for the exam is clear enough. Because this was the final component of the certificate, the university wanted to keep a 'traditional' closed exam in order to maintain rigour. I think they feel that because it has a closed exam, it makes the module – and the whole course – feel like a course would be if it was for regular full-time students instead of part-time adult students.

So as soon as the module started I began to keep telling the students about how the exam would be, that it would be entirely based on questions that we had covered in our weekly sessions, and that the marking was different – easier in a way – because these were essays that were being written in an exam, not at home on a coursework basis. We talked about exam techniques, about essay planning, about timing the writing – everything. We even had a mock exam one week where instead of a regular session I made the students write an essay in exam conditions. And afterwards we talked about how that went, how it felt and so on.

On the day itself, the group were sitting the exam in the same hall as lots of other students doing lots of other exams. There were only about 15 or so in the group, whereas in the hall as a whole there must have been 200 people – it was massive. I decided to go in early, so that I could talk to the group beforehand. I showed them where their seats were, where the toilets were, reassured them it would all go well. And about five minutes in, Charlotte just got up and ran out. By the time I got outside she was nowhere to be seen, and I only heard from her a couple of days later, when she sent me an email. We exchanged several emails and I did eventually find out what had happened.

Charlotte had always been a very challenging student to work with. At her best, she was capable of doing pretty good work in fact – certainly good enough for level 4 studies. But she was massively nervous, and lacking in confidence – cripplingly so. She'd left school at 15 with no O levels, and had generally had a bad time there, with teachers writing her off and one even telling her not to bother going in for her exams. So this was the first exam she'd done since then. She'd done the mock exam, but that was our regular room, just our group. When she walked into the hall and saw all of those desks, she just panicked and could not talk herself down. So after a few minutes of staring at a blank piece of paper, she felt that she couldn't handle it. So she left.

What do you think can be learned from this (true) story? What are the implications of Charlotte's story for Edward's professional practice, and are there any aspects of your own professional practice that might be changed in the light of this account? Some possible issues to consider might include:

- The appropriateness of the closed examination format. If an alternative mode of assessment can be found, then why not use it? Is there any intrinsic need for the use of closed exams?
- Charlotte's learning history. Should Edward have worked more extensively to learn about Charlotte's prior experiences of formal education?
- The exam room itself. Would a different room have helped? Large exam halls full of row upon row of tables and chairs can be intimidating for many students. If the exam had been held in a smaller room,

perhaps reserved solely for the history group, would Charlotte have been better able to cope?

- Overall, has Edward – and by extension, the adult education department – in any way failed to make any adjustments for Charlotte that could have been defined as 'reasonable'? Has Charlotte been discriminated against in any way?

Conclusion

The relationship between legislation, and social and attitudinal change, is complex at best. Undoubtedly, changing social and cultural attitudes have helped push an inclusive agenda into mainstream educational cultures and practices, spurred on by policy makers – and by education researchers as well. As teachers and trainers, we don't need to be policy experts – but it is useful for us to know about why it is framed in the ways that it is, and how it makes a difference to our everyday working lives.

A SUMMARY OF **KEY POINTS**

In this chapter we have looked at the following key points:

> **the ways in which shifts in government policy can impact on education practice in both the short and the long term;**

> **key pieces of legislation that have affected education provision during the last 30 years;**

> **the 2010 Equality Act, and the implications of the Act for providers of FE.**

REFERENCES AND FURTHER READING REFERENCES AND FURTHER READING

Books

Smith, C (2009) From special needs to inclusive education, in Sharp, J, Ward, S and Hankin, L (eds) *Education Studies: an issues-based approach*. Second edition. Exeter: Learning Matters.

Wright, A-M, Abdi-Jama, S, Colquhon, S, Speare, J and Partridge, T (2006) *FE Lecturer's Guide to Diversity and Inclusion*. London: Continuum.

Journal articles

Warwick, I, Maxwell, C, Statham, J, Aggleton, P and Simon, A (2008) Supporting mental health and emotional well-being among younger students in Further Education. *Journal of Further and Higher Education*, 32(1): 1–13.

Websites

The official press release relating to the Wolf review of vocational education is at:

www.education.gov.uk/inthenews/pressnotices/a0075181/wolf-review-proposes-major-reform-of-vocational-education

The 2010 Equality Act can be found at:

www.legislation.gov.uk/ukpga/2010/15/part/6/chapter/2

Index